BIPOLAR DISORDER

How to Live an Empowered Life With Bipolar

(Learn the Symptoms and Strategies on How You Can Cope)

Janice Shelton

Published By Janice Shelton

Janice Shelton

All Rights Reserved

Bipolar Disorder: How to Live an Empowered Life With Bipolar (Learn the Symptoms and Strategies on How You Can Cope)

ISBN 978-1-77485-386-3

Legal & Disclaimer

The information contained in this book is not designed to replace or take the place of any form of medicine or professional medical advice. The information in this book has been provided for educational and entertainment purposes only.

The information contained in this book has been compiled from sources deemed reliable, and it is accurate to the best of the Author's knowledge; however, the Author cannot guarantee its accuracy and validity and cannot be held liable for any errors or omissions. Changes are periodically made to this book. You must consult your doctor or get professional medical advice before using any of the suggested remedies, techniques, or information in this book.

TABLE OF CONTENTS

Introduction

Greetings! I would like to thank everyone who purchased this book. I hope to provide the best guidance and information possible about Bipolar Disorder. Bipolar disorder (or manic-depressive disease) is a brain disorder. This brain disorder produces symptoms such as abnormal energy levels, activity levels, and inability to deal with daily responsibilities. Although all people experience this symptom occasionally, it is more severe and intense.

Even more, these symptoms could have a negative affect on every aspect of your life including your academics as well as your work and your relationships. Bipolar Disorder, like other disorders, can be treated and managed. People suffering from it can enjoy a happy and healthy life, with minimal stress.

Bipolar disorder symptoms affect most people before they reach age 25. However, it can also occur in adolescents and young adults. Some people might experience symptoms even as young children.

Bipolar disorder has many triggers that are not fully understood. But, the majority of doctors believe it to be hereditary.

Bipolar disorder is often not diagnosed correctly or treated appropriately.

This book is designed to assist you in managing your Bipolar disorder and other extreme symptoms.

This book will describe the signs and symptom of bipolar disorder. The causes of the disorder, their treatments, and their benefits. And how to live with the disorder.

I hope that you will find this book useful in understanding bipolar disorder.

However, this book is not meant to be your sole source of information for treatment or support. If you feel you might have bipolar disorder you should consult a professional and talk with a trusted friend. It is vital to seek professional help and to talk to someone you trust to help you.

Chapter 1: Why Meds Don't Suffice

You'll remember that when you were first diagnosed with bipolar disorder, your psychiatrist or psychologist prescribed you a couple of pills. Although medication can help with bipolar control, they're not the cure. For most people, they are just helpful. Although it is popular to believe that magic pills can solve all problems, the truth is that they are rarely that easy to use. The vast majority of people will spend years trying out different combinations of drugs to find the one that works best. It's like working as a scientist in an laboratory. You will never know what works until you try.

It doesn't always Work

The medical industry is full of customers. They aren't worried if they get you better.

Because you will likely still have gaps in treatment that medication cannot address, it is important to explore alternative methods. It is important to encourage routine and self regulation in order to manage your disease effectively. It is possible to "beat" this condition by having the willpower of self-control.

When self-management is combined with medication it can be like a double blow. You are not only getting the chemical help you brain needs, but also controlling your symptoms when that doesn't work. It's a good way to help yourself, and it also helps you avoid doctors who think pills can solve everything (something you will firsthand discover is false).

There will be days when bipolar symptoms are severe. These tools allow you to be in control when you are suffering from manic episodes. There may be times when your medication is not available. In these cases, you won't be able to help yourself.

Side Effects

Extreme side effects can sometimes be a reason patients stop taking their medications. Sometimes, they are even worse than what the medication is supposed to treat. Some side effects can cause the symptoms to worsen, so even if you have never been in suicidal thoughts, you could be suffering from this medication. This is due to the "pick and match" mental health medication approach. The fact that there is almost always a single cause of depression aside from chemical imbalance makes it difficult to make the right choice. This can result in months of painful side effects and little relief.

Not Just Mental

Bipolar depression is a severe mental disorder that many people don't know. Different brains have different receptors, and research has shown this. These receptors enable your brain to respond to different chemicals or hormones. One of these chemicals includes serotonin. The mood and mental health of serotonin as well as norepinephrine and dopamine is all affected by them. They're also called "feel-good" chemicals. Endorphins also have the ability to affect your mood. These hormones are released if your body feels happy. You can trick the brain into releasing endorphins to give you a temporary boost.

These medications fix chemical imbalances. But how can you trick your brain with medication?

Medication works by blocking the brain's reuptake, but it also controls the huge upswing. Most stabilizers only do one thing: They work to maintain the chemical balance rather than constantly changing them. Because Lithium only works in the manic stages, it isn't considered a stabilizer.

So, what other options can you use to stabilize your hormonal swings than medication?

Chapter 2: Understanding Bipolar Disorder

There is nothing wrong with mood swings. People experience times when they feel happy but then feel depressed. Now think about a normal mood swing. Then multiply that number by several. This is bipolar disorder. Sometimes, these mood swings can be so severe it can have a negative impact on a person's career or personal relationships. Some even resort to suicide when their mind cannot cope with the stress.

If your moods are becoming out of control and you are experiencing negative emotions, you may have bipolar disorder. So you can get the medical care you need, you should learn everything you can about bipolar disorder.

What is Bipolar Disorder (Bipolar Disorder)?

Bipolar disorder can be described as a brain condition that causes episodes of mood swings in which the person's moods change from one extreme, high-energy state to another. These moods seem so unlike each other, that they are called bipolar. These extreme manic/depressive episodes last only a few days to weeks, with regular periods in between. But in extreme cases, they can last several months and can often lead to severe health impairment.

Bipolar disorder is different from other mental health conditions. People have only recently become aware of it. Around 70% of people who do have the disorder don't get an accurate diagnosis.

The majority of people who experience bipolar disorder have experienced a depression prior to experiencing their manic episodes. However, some may only experience hypomania. The majority of people who experience depression first need to seek professional help. This compares with those who experience manic episodes first. Almost all people don't realize that they have a problem. If you suspect that you may develop bipolar disorder, you should be screened and monitored to ensure that you take control of the situation before it becomes serious.

Bipolar Disorders in Different Types

Diagnosing bipolar disorder can be tricky because of the three types you must watch out for.

Bipolar I: This is the classic bipolar disorder. Many people think this is the best. This type is characterised by at least one mixed episode or manic and, most often, one depressive.

Bipolar II. In this case, the patient does not experience full-blown episodes of manic depression like in Bipolar 1. This type bipolar disorder sees the sufferer experience mild to severe episodes of manic depression and hypomania. This type is often misdiagnosed to be depression as the sufferer doesn't seem to notice the manic episodes.

Cyclothymia, a mild bipolar disorder that causes mild episodes of depression and hypomania in a person with cyclical periods of the condition. Cyclothymia patients are more likely to not seek help than those with full-blown bipolar disorder. Their symptoms are milder than full-blown depression, and so they don't impact their quality or life.

Bipolar Disorders: What Causes It?

Bipolar disorder has no single cause. This makes the diagnosis more difficult. While some people may be predisposed to develop bipolar disorder, not everyone does. Research shows that an abnormal thyroid function and a faulty biologic clock can make someone more prone for manic depression episodes.

Also, there are psychological and other factors that may trigger the development of bipolar disorder.

Over-stress - If someone is genetically predisposed for bipolar disorder, high levels of stress could make it happen. The majority of people can experience manic or depression episodes when they are confronted with life-changing events such a marriage, moving away from home or the death a close friend.

Substance abuse. Despite inconclusive research linking substance abuse with bipolar disorders, there has been evidence that it makes existing conditions worse. Ecstasy, cocaine, and ecstasy have been shown to increase the severity and intensity of manic episodes. Similarly, depressants like alcohol or tranquilizers can make depression worse.

Sleep deprivation- As it was stated earlier, sudden changes in a person's biological time can trigger bipolar disorder. In other words, not getting enough sleep at nights can disrupt your circadian rhythm.

Medication – Certain prescription drugs, including antidepressants may also cause bipolar manic episodes. Some medications such as antidepressants, thyroid medications, appetite suppressants and caffeine can prolong a person's manic episodes and make them feel more intense.

Seasonal changes – Bipolar disorder patients who are susceptible to depressive episodes and manic episodes have been known to experience seasonal changes. The spring and summer are thought to trigger manic episodes, while the colder periods of the year may cause depressive mood swings.

Common myths and misconceptions about Bipolar Disorder

People with bipolar disorder often switch between manic and depression. However, this is not a typical feature of the disorder. Some sufferers experience depression less frequently and for longer durations than manias. Other people may be unaware of their manic symptoms until they become severe.

Bipolar disorder has a few side effects. It can affect moods. However, most people do not realize the extent of it. People suffering from bipolar disorder are often low in energy and have reduced sex drives. They also have difficulty concentrating and making smart decisions. There is also evidence that bipolar disorder is linked to the development or chronic illnesses such as heart disease, diabetes, and other conditions.

The only thing you can do to manage bipolar disorder is to take medication. It is possible to drastically reduce the symptoms of manic/depressive episodes through exercise, healthy eating and avoiding stressful activities.

People with bipolar disorder are unable to live normal, healthy life. However, there are ways to overcome this condition. There is hope for bipolar disorder patients.

It is important to understand this mental condition before you can make any progress towards recovery. You need to know if you think you might have bipolar disorder.

Chapter 3: What Is Bipolar Disorder, And How Can It Be Treated?

Research has revealed that bipolar disorder is caused by an imbalance of neurotransmitters in the brain. This evidence supports the theory. While it is unclear what the causes or causes of the illness are, it's well-known that environmental, genetic, and biochemical factors all play an important role in the development of the disorder. Important to note that bipolar disorder patients have a high incidence of manic episodes and depression. Other conditions, hormonal imbalances as well as stress and drug abuse can cause this, as well as other health problems. Bipolar disorder is often an inheritable condition that runs in the family, according to research. Certain stressful events may trigger the symptoms of bipolar disorder and act as triggers.

Why it is so important to recognize mania

This is something you need to be aware of. Treating bipolar disorders is something most people overlook. Mania may be life-threatening if it is not treated. Let us take the example Agnes, who was suffering from manic symptoms and was involved in a serious car accident. Agnes drove at a high speed because she considered herself a race car driver. One man who was suffering from mania had invested all his life savings into the stock market in an impulsive manner and ended up losing it all. These are just two examples of bipolar disorder. Although the behavior may be different in each case, it is common for them to all be untreated.

Remember that even erratic behaviors do not necessarily signify you are bipolar. It is important that you seek immediate medical attention if your symptoms or behaviors continue for more than seven days. The worst thing about this is that most people put off seeking professional help or treatment for long periods of time. Bipolar disorder usually takes ten to twelve years for diagnosis. This indicates that there is a real risk of developing bipolar disorder as long as the disease remains undiagnosed, untreated, or even partially treated. Research has shown that bipolar patients have more than 20 % of those who commit suicide without proper treatment.

Bipolar disorder in the Family Line

While the exact cause of bipolar disorder is still unknown, numerous medical reports as well as research suggest that it is hereditary. Statistics prove that approximately 2/3 of bipolar disorder sufferers have at most one relative with the same illness. This indicates that bipolar disorder may be genetic and runs in families.

Although bipolar disorder is a condition that can be inherited, it cannot be predicted how it will affect other members of your family. You should consult a physician if there is any concern. By doing this, you can have your questions answered as well as screening for mood disorder during your annual check-ups. DBSA recommends that all people be screened for bipolar disorder regardless of family history.

Bipolar disorder among children

It is alarming to realize the absence of research about the onset of bipolar disorders in childhood. Unfortunately, the disease has been recognized in children as young a three-year-old. Many more children have been discovered to suffer from bipolar disorder. Additionally, symptoms of bipolar disorder can develop as early as childhood. Research has found that mothers with bipolar disorder have described their children as having trouble sleeping and exhibiting difficult behaviors. In some cases, children seemed more clingy than normal. Bipolar children also exhibit extreme anger, tantrums, seizures and other symptoms. Sometimes, they may be even more angry if you say "no" when you don't want to do something that interests them.

Similar to clinical depression, parents need to be aware that if their child has been diagnosed with bipolar disorder they should seek medical attention immediately. The early diagnosis of bipolar disorder is important for children, especially if they have a mood disorder.

Chapter 4: Mania And Depression

Therapy looks for two key components in bipolar patients: depression and mania. We covered the most common symptoms that indicate a person is suffering from a manic, hypomanic or depressive episode. We will be discussing the diagnostic basis for each type extreme mood episode experienced by bipolar patients in this chapter.

Mania

Beyond elation and euphoria, the term mania can also mean irritability, arousal, persistent energy, or persistent elation. Experts agree that the opposite mood to depression is mania.

While a manic episode or two is sufficient to make a diagnosis of bipolar disorder, the patient must also rule out other possible causes. Some stimulant drugs, like anti-depressants and methamphetamines may cause manic episodes.

Experts suggest that the best time to treatmania is in the early stages. Patients can become resistant to treatment and may refuse to accept it. Even if depression is absent, patients often experience mood swings that can be triggered by disrupted sleep patterns or stress from environmental factors.

Psychosis, hallucinations (delusions of grandeur), and catatonia are common signs of manic episodes. Aggressive behavior and grand plotting are indicators of manic episodes.

Even though mild cases, or hypomania, of mania may not be as severe, they can still present as a barrier to normal daily living. Hypomania can be associated with creative outbursts and artistic tendencies in certain cases. Many people are unaware they have it. While many well-known actors, writers, and artists are frequently considered bipolar as a result, many were creative geniuses.

A bipolar disorder that is not properly diagnosed can lead to the mistaken identification of an addict. It is often true that only those with some level of self control and awareness of the effects of their condition on their lives will seek treatment. These people are very rare compared to patients who lack self-control.

Depression

Depression is not like mania. It refers, instead of mania, to an extreme low mood and energy that often affects a person's capacity to function normally. While mania is usually associated with bipolar disorders, depression is considered a medical condition known as clinical depression. It is not necessarily a psychological illness.

Individuals with depression often experience overwhelming feelings of sadness, anxiety or emptiness. They may feel guilt, worthlessness or irritability frequently. People who are depressed or suffer from depression often lose interest the things they used to enjoy.

Depressive episodes resulting from bipolar disorder must be ruled out by first looking at the recent events that might have triggered them. Depression can be a normal response for life-changing situations such as the death, financial difficulties, or injuries.

Bipolar disorder is not the only mental disorder that may show signs of depression. Major depression, dysthymia and chronic depression are also possible. Depressive episodes may also be caused by trauma and anxiety disorders.

Diagnostically diagnosing bipolar disorder only on the basis that it is depressive disorders can prove difficult because there are other possible diagnoses and sometimes hypomanic episodes may go unreported. Experts believe there are many misdiagnosed cases. The reason is that patients with bipolar disorder don't experience manic episodes but have mild hypomania.

Manic-Depressive Episodes

As stated in the previous chapter, bipolars are able to experience mania and depression at the same time. Mixed episodes, as they're called, can be either dominantly depressive or dominantlymaniac.

Mixed episodes are dangerous because they can make patients feel more confused and cause rapid cycle of moods. They are usually accompanied psychosis, grandiose illusions, and may lead to the patient getting hurt.

Patients with mixed episodes must not be left unattended. They need closer supervision and attention than patients who are only experiencing hypomania or other primary types bipolar episodes.

Chapter 5: What To Do When You See A Physician?

This list will allow you to quickly determine if your symptoms are normal or if it is possible that you might be suffering from bipolar disorder. It is better that you consult your doctor as soon as you feel the need. Unfortunately, some people would rather keep things the same even if something is wrong. Some will even pretend that they don't have the symptoms of bipolar disorders.

It is incorrect to believe that bipolar disorder will improve on its' own and that you don't need treatment. However, many people suffer from extreme mood swings and mood swings. These people will often ignore their symptoms and pretend that they are normal. Many fail notice they already have symptoms. Failure to act on the problem and take appropriate action can cause instability. A doctor is essential to prevent you from suffering more problems and worsening your health.

For your mental well-being, you need to see a certified and reliable mental health provider. These professionals are well-versed in managing patients suffering from bipolar disorder. As such, they can manage your symptoms.

If you are still reluctant to have treatment, you can always talk with a close friend. You can also speak to your trusted health professional or another person who you are familiar with and you trust. At the least, this is a first step. Be aware that the first step can be very difficult. But, once you've received the appropriate treatment or prescription medication, you can avoid more severe episodes.

What to Do If You Suicide Attempts

People with bipolar disorder could experience suicidal thoughts. It is possible to become suicidal if someone already has these kinds of thoughts. These are often common. It is important to do the following for anyone who may be in this same situation.

Contact a friend/family member

Get professional help from your doctor.

Reach out to a suicide hotline. You can reach the National Suicide Prevention Lifeline at 800-8255.

If you need emergency help for someone you love, or if suicide attempt is imminent, dial 911.

There is also a risk of bipolar disorder.

Bipolar Disorder and Its Associated Complications

Bipolar disorder patients are also more likely be diagnosed with other conditions. This is why it is so important that you seek the necessary treatment as soon as possible. If you have bipolar disorder, the following conditions may occur:

ADHD or Attention Deficit Hyperactivity Disorder

Bipolar disorder has no known cause. Bipolar disorder can be caused by many factors. These triggering factors can lead to bipolar episodes. It is therefore important that people are aware of them. These factors include:

Neurotransmitters are brain chemicals that can cause mood swings as well as bipolar disorder. Neurotransmitters (brain chemicals) can naturally occur within the brain.

Hormones may also trigger bipolar disorder. Your hormones affect your moods.

Bipolar episodes may also occur due to environmental factors. Stress, trauma, abuse and other factors can all play a role. All factors can contribute.

Genes: As with any other medical condition and disorder, bipolar disorder may also be due to genes. If your family member has bipolar disorder, it's possible you might also have it.

Bipolar Disorder and Risk Factors

This condition is not only caused by the above-mentioned causes, but there are also other factors that could increase the risk of developing bipolar disorder.

Long periods of stress

Major life events or changes

Abuse of drugs and alcohol

Parents or siblings diagnosed with bipolar disorder

In the early 20s, ADHD symptoms are more common in those with Attention-Deficiency Disorder Hyperactivity (also known by bipolar disorder and ADHD). This is how it can be hard to tell whether someone is suffering either from ADHD or bipolar disorders. It is possible to have ADHD and bipolar disorder in certain cases.

Anxiety disorders

Anxiety disorders may increase your risk of developing bipolar disease. You may also be more likely to develop bipolar disorder if your anxiety disorders are related to post-traumatic stress disorder, or phobias.

Health Problems

People who suffer from bipolar disorder might also be experiencing health problems. Obesity increases the risk of this condition. Other health problems include heart disease and thyroid problems.

Addictions

Individuals with an addiction to certain substances can also make the problem worse. Many sufferers of this condition have problems with their drug, cigarette, and alcohol use. While it might seem like drugs can help, there are worse episodes of bipolar that can be deadly.

Bipolar Disorder: The complications

The person suffering from bipolar disorder needs to get help immediately. But, it is possible for someone with bipolar disorder to refuse treatment or not admit that they have it. If you do not treat bipolar disorder it can have negative and serious consequences in your daily life. Below are the potential complications of bipolar disorder if not treated.

Problems in relationships with friends and colleagues

Poor performance at school or in work

The individual may show suicidal tendencies.

Experience financial problems

Legal problems

Extreme loneliness

Substance abuse/addiction

Diagnosis and Tests

After your doctor suspects you have bipolar disorder you will need to undergo certain diagnostic procedures and tests. These tests will be used to determine whether you are suffering from bipolar disorder.

Physical Exam

Like any other disease or illness you may have, the physical exam is necessary. This will serve as the first step in determining your height, weight, and other vital signs. Your doctor will take vital signs such as your body temperature and blood pressure. Your doctor will keep track of these details so that they can be used later for analysis or diagnosis.

Laboratory tests

After the physical exam, lab tests will be performed. To examine the causes of your symptoms, you'll need to undergo blood and urine testing.

Psychological Assessment

Aside from the physical exam and lab tests your doctor will also ask specific questions about your feelings, thoughts, and behaviour. The questionnaire will ask you to complete. You can also be asked by your doctor to provide information about your loved ones, provided that you have given your permission.

Daily Record of Your Moods

Motility charting is used to aid the doctor assess and evaluate what you are experiencing. Your doctor will track and examine your mood data every day. To assist in the diagnosis and treatment, this chart tracks your moods and even your sleep patterns.

Chapter 6: The Psychology Of Psychotherapy

Research into bipolar disorder has shown that patients who are treated with both medication and therapy are more likely get better quickly and to avoid relapse. Therapy can teach how to address the problems that your symptoms are causing. Therapy can also address other issues such as anxiety, substance abuse, and relationship problems.

Highly trained professionals in mental health can:

Interventions in early manic and depression episodes can reduce severity.

Monitor the patient's current status

Assist in drug compliance

Teach patients how they can recognize and manage depressive or manic symptoms.

Educate patients and offer treatment.

Psychotherapy can also be a helpful tool for patients.

Take care of your feelings of sadness and inadequacy

Cope and accept guilt and regret after manic episodes

It is essential to adjust to the reality of the illness, understand the adverse effects of manic episodes, and especially to patients who believe their mania to have creative, exhilarating or positive qualities.

Cognitive-Behavioral Therapy

CBT, or cognitive-behavioral therapy, may prove to be especially helpful for patients. CBT or cognitive-behavioral treatment is a well-structured and conscious technique that helps the patient understand his negative thoughts, behavior patterns, and how to change them. CBT is also useful for treating mood disorders such anxiety or depression. Studies show that CBT is very beneficial for patients with bipolar disorder. CBT has the following benefits for patients with bipolar disorder:

It is important to recognize manic episodes and modify your behavior when they occur.

Find ways to combat depression.

Family Therapy

Parents, siblings, or both, should participate in therapy for bipolar patients. Therapy can help them understand how to deal bipolar symptoms, the need of medication, and how best to manage episodes. There are several recommendations to support the patient.

As a first step, make a treatment plan. The patient and the family must sign this contract.

Bipolar disorder and alcoholism are not the same thing. The patient's bipolar disorder can be dissimilar to alcoholism. Therefore, it is important that family members support their loved one. You can help by being compassionate and listening carefully.

Encourage the patient and encourage compliance. If the patient fails, force hospitalization can be used.

Always ready and available to refer the psychiatrist authorized for the treatment of the patient.

Family members shouldn't feel guilty, and the patient shouldn't feel guilty.

Bipolar disorder can impact the family members as well. Family members should learn how to take care themselves and reduce anxiety and stress associated with the illness. Internet support groups, message boards, and forums can be very helpful for caregivers.

Interpersonal, Social Rhythm Therapy

This type of therapy helps reduces stress in the patient's life and because stress is a trigger for bipolar disorder, this relationship-centered approach can help lower mood cycling. Interpersonal Therapy focuses on patient's current relationships and helps them improve their relationships with important people. IPSRT focuses primarily in maintaining a schedule of daily activities to reduce triggers, and improve emotional stability. Patients can also learn to avoid conflicts in their personal relationships through IPSRT. Initial evidence suggests that IPSRT with medication may help prevent more manic episodes.

Chapter 7: Diagnosis

The hardest thing about this type of disorder is the diagnosis. People who have this disorder won't want anything to do it with a doctor or psychiatrist. Therefore, they will choose to ignore the attempts to help and turn their backs on the doctors. It may take family members to spot the problem early on and provide the support needed to help the person with the disorder. They won't go in by themselves because they don't know if they have any problems.

Once you get the person with a disorder to come in, the diagnosis is going to be made based upon the assessment performed at the clinic. This is done by a professional of psychological health. Presenting the different criteria of the disorder is the best way to do so. This will get them involved in the healing process and make it more likely. Doctors are often not able to evaluate the patient on their own. They may need to consult with others to help determine if they have the right characteristics.

You can make it easier for someone with this kind of disorder, such as a child, to help you diagnose the condition. Some doctors decide it is better not to tell their patients. While this is one route, there is plenty of research to support the idea that the patient should be informed about the condition to receive the best treatment.

During the evaluation, the patient may be asked questions about their symptoms. Some questions may be asked to determine how these symptoms affect their daily life. The doctor will be looking into any thoughts or feelings that may lead to harm to others, self-harm experiences, and thoughts of suicide.

The doctor will use the information the patient has provided at the sessions to make a diagnosis. These two factors can often be combined to give a good view of what is going. There are some tests that can help to determine if someone has borderline personality disorder. To rule out possible causes, lab tests and a physical examination may be required.

Once the condition has been identified and diagnosed in the patient, it is time for treatment. Although it may be time-consuming and a lot of work, this is necessary to restore sanity and happiness to the individual. Here are some tips on how to diagnose the disorder and how to get help so that you feel better quickly.

International Classifications

There are several classifications that can be found that are internationally accepted to aid with diagnosis. These classifications allow the clinician to perform the diagnosis without having any personal beliefs. Everything can stay the same throughout. The World Health Organization recognizes borderline personality disorder. Then, it is divided into two more categories that we'll be discussing a bit later.

Impulsive Type

The impulsive category is the first to be identified in this list. Three of the items below must be present for someone to be diagnosed as this disorder.

A tendency to act out, or to get out from under control. This is going to happen by accident and it will not be caused by someone forcing the person to act. It is common for the person to do the act and not think about what might happen. They will just do it because they have a little disagreement.

Patients with this condition will often exhibit a tendency toward quarrelsome behavior, which can lead to conflicts with others. This is especially true if the patient has been criticised or stopped from engaging in impulsive behavior. These people are those who fight with others regularly and use any slight as an excuse.

An issue is having violent or angry outbursts. These individuals are not only experiencing these issues, but they lack the ability or the will to deal with the resulting explosions and other issues. They will seem angry, but they also will not be able calmly return to normal.

These people may have trouble staying on track if they don't receive immediate reward. They may have been passionate about the idea and were willing to do it even if it didn't provide them with immediate rewards. If this happened, they are likely to get angry and frustrated and abandon it. This is a common occurrence. A person will only keep going with what they know they can do and will be rewarded.

These people tend to be unstable and unpredictable in their moods. This can make it hard to keep up.

These are the five symptoms that can be seen in people with an impulsive disorder. You will notice that they do not think about the consequences of their actions or how they might affect others. At least three of the above items must be present for a person to be diagnosed.

Type of borderline

The next step is the borderline. This one will be different. This will combine a lot of what you have seen above with a few things from the following list. To be considered for this diagnosis, you will need to show at least three symptoms of the impulsive type. Here are some things to look out for:

The person with this personality type will often be uncertain about their self image, internal preferences, and aims in life. They don't feel valued and are unable to connect with others. They may be confused or wander around aimlessly because they don't know who, what, where, and how they should live their lives.

They could also be more likely to get involved in unhealthy and intense relationships. This includes those who meet and then marry within a few months. It doesn't necessarily have to last that long. The relationship is too unstable to last and was very intense, so it is likely to lead to an emotional crisis.

They will do everything possible to avoid being abandoned. They are scared of the day when they will not have anyone to call on for support or their friends. They push others away, and they don't always see the bigger picture. They will work nearly obsessively to make certain that others do the same for them, so that they can always have the companionship and help that they need.

They may be subject to self-harm, as well as threats. This is usually not done to manipulate someone or change their feelings. This is more an act of self-harm in the hope of controlling their emotions. They will struggle with their emotions and could resort to self-harm if they don't get the relief they need.

A lot of people feel empty. They will feel empty as they do not have any plans for the future and do not know what they want to do. They don't have any long-term goals. They just want to be happy. This can lead you to a rather empty life.

They will display an impulsive and erratic behavior. This will include speeding and substance abuse. The purpose of these activities is to help the sufferer get some relief from their uncontrolled emotions or bad feelings. The problem is when they start to feel guilty about what they have done and feel even worse.

As stated before, there are a lot of factors that must be met before someone is diagnosed with this type. All who meet these requirements need to get the help they deserve as soon as they can.

Millon's Subtypes

We'll first take a look to see the different subtypes involved in borderline personality disorder. Theodore Millon previously suggested that there are four subtypes for borderline personality disorder. The person with this disorder will often exhibit one or more the following features. These include the subtypes as well as the features.

Discouraged - This subtype can also have the features that are avoidant. The person in this category feels powerless and helpless.

Petulant-This category also contains the traits of someone who is very critical of what is going on around them. These people are often disillusioned and can quickly be slighted.

Impulsive-This category includes those who are very antisocial and do not want to be with others. These features include someone who is likely to commit suicide, someone who is easily irritable and gloomy and who can sometimes become agitated. These people are likely to be anxious, disorganized, flighty or superficially impulsive, and fear losing their possessions.

Self-destructive--this category is also going to include the features of someone is very masochistic or depressive. They will become very moody and hyperactive and they will start to lose many of the positive aspects that make them unique. They are averse to change and are prone to becoming deferential or conforming.

It is possible to have more than one type of disorder.

While there are many theories and opinions about this disorder, the majority of them will be able to help you understand what's going on. It isn't a straightforward diagnosis. There is no one way to sum up what is happening for every case. Some cases will be affected by abuse from the past. However, that does not mean they will develop this disorder. It can be difficult to manage this disorder because there are so many things that must be done before it appears.

Even people who have been trained to treat this type can find it difficult to diagnose. This can lead to the patient not receiving the proper help. However, these definitions will give you a good start point. A professional can also use experience and training to diagnose you so you get the help you need.

Family Members

You can diagnose someone with this disorder even by how they treat their family members. People with this disorder tend to be less friendly to their family members. They also feel more angry at the same people. People with this disorder often try to get away from their family because they are angry at someone or concerned about how they will be perceived by the family. A lot of times the family will feel helpless and angry over the way this person is treating them.

In 2003, there was a study that showed that family members will change their thinking once they realize the cause. Most people with the disorder experience anger and feelings of hurt once they understand their situation. This might not seem like something that would occur, but many people believe these feelings are caused by the fact that the family was given incorrect information about their disorder. They are now blaming them for the problem.

Families should learn as much about the disorder as possible to be able help their loved ones. While this may seem like a good way to begin to learn about the disorder, you'll soon discover that it is often inaccurate. Find the right information. It will make it easier to understand what you and your loved one are seeing.

This will be equally hard for loved ones as it will for the person experiencing the problem. They are the ones who have been emotionally damaged by their loved-one's insistence on not having anything to do. The family must receive the therapy and support needed to get better grips on the situation. It can be easier to come together and get through this situation if you know the details and how they affect the family.

Chapter 8: Maintain Sleep Hygiene

It is vital to practice good sleep hygiene in order to manage bipolar disorder. Sometimes, poor sleep habits can trigger bipolar disorder. Good sleep habits can help to reduce mood cycles.

Tip 1

It will help you sleep better by getting in tune with your body's natural cycles of sleep and wakefulness. Here are some guidelines.

Wake up at the same times as you go to bed. This helps your body set its internal clock and optimizes your sleep quality. Find a time during the night when it is easy to feel tired and restful. On weekends, the same time you go to bed every night is best. If you feel you are getting enough rest at night, you can go to bed at the same hour every morning.

Napping is not recommended if you have trouble sleeping at nights.

Tip #2: Be aware of your light exposure

The hormone melatonin naturally occurs in your body and helps regulate your night-wake cycle. Light exposure is what causes melatonin to be produced. There are some things that you can do in order for your melatonin production to be balanced.

During the course of the day

Bright sunlight in the morning is possible by getting up earlier in the morning. Get the morning sunshine by doing yoga or drinking tea outside on your balcony. You can eat your breakfast right next to a sunny window.

Spend more daylight time outside: Walking your dog regularly or going for a walk outside will help you get more sunlight.

Working near a sunlit window will allow you to receive the maximum amount of natural light. Use a light-therapy box if necessary.

Evening

Be sure to stop watching TV or using your phone and laptop before bed. Disruptive blue light from your TV, tablet phone, computer and phone is especially evident. Software such as f.lux can be used.

About eReaders. E-readers are more disruptive than ereaders who don't have a light source. This problem can be solved if you read printed books.

If you want to make your bedroom dark, consider using a sleep mask. It is best to cover electronics that emit sunlight.

Along with the above recommendations, you should avoid caffeine, nicotine, alcohol, and large meals before bed. Your bedroom should be kept cool and peaceful. You should also keep the noise down.

Sleep aids

Before you start using any sleep aids consult your doctor. Bipolar patients are able to use drugs such as benzodiazepines, but only for a limited time. You should be aware that sleeping aids can have side effect such as:

They are very addictive

Drugs may cause aggressive or hostile behavior in certain cases.

They can lead to sleepiness, amnesia, and coordination problems.

You shouldn't mix them with alcohol.

Chapter 9: Learn How You Can Deal With Things That Will Stress Your Mind Out

The stressors in our daily lives can make a big difference in how this disorder affects us. It was also found that you can avoid an attack or episode by controlling your stress levels.

People with bipolar disorder are like any other person. They worry about the future of their families and finances, as well as their health. You can manage and control stress by using your God-given skills to address the daily problems in your lives.

This chapter will help you learn how to manage your stress so that you have fewer depressive attacks and more manic episodes.

How to cope with your stressors

Step 1: Identify Your Stressors. You have a lot of options to identify the source of a problem.

Internal signals can be changes in your body, such as tension and headaches, breathing difficulties, or tension in your chest. These changes can be signs that stress is brewing and can alert you to the need for immediate attention. Emotional changes such as anxiety, depression, and hopelessness can also be observed. These changes in your emotions could indicate that you have unsolved issues.

Step two: Prioritize Your Issues. People with bipolar disorder often experience major problems after depressive episodes or dramatic manic episodes. Due to your low motivation and constant fatigue during depressive episodes, you may face financial difficulties.

Also, manic episodes can cause you to shop excessively and can result in financial difficulties that you will need help with once the episode is over. It can be difficult to feel hopeless, overwhelmed and frustrated when you realize the gravity and scope of your problems. You may even feel like it is impossible to solve your problems, especially if you are unable to find the right solution.

Step 3: Determine what your Coping Resources are. Your coping resource is a combination of internal and external resources that can help you solve the priority issues you have identified. Your external resources or assets include support from people who understand you, such as your doctor, family members and coworkers.

Other people, including support agencies and your financial assets, may also be available to offer support. Your internal resources and intelligence include your creativity, creativity, determinations, ingenuity sense of humor, compassion, and other skills.

Step Four: Determine the Causes of Your Problems. It is likely that you will face stumblingblocks in your efforts to deal with your problems. These stumbling stops can be internal or external. Your own stumbling stones must be identified so that you can eliminate them and solve your problems.

Step Five: Overcome the Obstacles Blocking Your Coping Ressources. After you have identified your own stumblingblocks, it is essential that you confront them and come up with solutions. You might need to challenge your own beliefs in order for you to move past your stumblingblocks. Always remember that it's okay to seek help and advice from other people.

Chapter 10: Who Is At Risk?

You can be at-risk for this disorder. Bipolar I can be more common than bipolar 2, but it is less common. Reports of bipolar 1 in the United States are about 1%. Bipolar disorders affect both men and their spouses equally. Women are more likely to suffer from depressive symptoms, however. It is believed that bipolar disorder begins before the age of 25. However, it is becoming more common among children and teenagers.

Bipolar I is the most severe form mental illness. People suffering from this disorder have trouble functioning at work so they usually stay unemployed. In addition to this, bipolar I disorders require that most people be hospitalized. People suffering from bipolar I and/or bipolar II disorders are likely to commit suicide.

Bipolar disorder is associated positively with creativity. People with this disorder are often productive, even during their manic episodes. They are determined to finish their tasks. Mania is when the symptoms become severe and the person becomes overwhelmed and must be hospitalized. People with bipolar disorder may experience episodes of mania, which can lead to them being unable to express their creative side.

Below is a list that gives you an idea of what bipolar disorder can do to anyone.

Ludwig van Beethoven, composer and pianist (as suggested)

Andy Behrman is author of Electroboy: Memoirs of Mania

John Clare, poet

Charles Dickens, author

Patty Duke, actress

Carrie Fisher, actor and writer

Mel Gibson, actor & director

JeaneClaude Van Damme - actor

Amy Winehouse, musician

Virginia Woolfe, writer

This also shows the duality of affective state and creativity is beneficial. These people didn't allow their illness to hinder their talents and were able showcase their talent to the entire world.

Bipolar disorder could cause unproductivity at work and conflict between relationships. But with the right strategies, people can manage their illness (and sometimes even cure it).

Chapter 11: What Bipolar Disorder

Does Not Look Like

In order for people to get the correct treatment, they may need to be able to differentiate bipolar disorder from signs and symptoms similar to it. There are many mood swings that can occur, but not all of them are bipolar. Every person will have their good and poor days. These mood swings are sometimes a natural response to life's events. But, there are times when they are triggered by something. Bipolar disorder and unipolar depressive disorder are distinguished by hypomanic, manic, and mixed episodes.

Bipolar disorder could also be mistakenly misdiagnosed as schizophrenia, which is a condition that involves psychosis. Schizophrenia refers to episodes of psychotic symptoms including hallucinations. Delusions and disordered behavior. However, rather than experiencing intense moods, people with schizophrenia experience duller moods. Psychotic symptoms aren't limited to those with schizophrenia.

Bipolar disorder often gets confused with schizophrenia, which can also include mood and psychotic symptoms. The key difference is that in bipolar disorders, psychotic signs only appear when mood symptoms are present, while in schizoaffective disorders, psychotic effects can occur both when mood symptoms exist and for at least two consecutive weeks.

Borderline personality disorder is known for mood swings. But they are not nearly as common as bipolar disorder. Also, they tend to last less and are less noticeable than bipolar disorder. Borderline personality is characterized by mood swings. These mood swings occur as a response to events and can be linked with certain personality characteristics.

Some symptoms of bipolar disorder may be temporarily mimicked by intoxication from certain drugs. But the effects of these substances wear off very quickly, and they do not cause bipolar disorder. Bipolar disorder can also mimic symptoms of certain medical conditions like hypothyroidism and multiple sclerosis. Proper treatment requires a precise diagnosis of bipolar disorders.

Types Of Bipolar Disorder

Different people have different bipolar disorders. They experience different types of episodes. Other types include cyclothymic and bipolar disorder that is not otherwise specified (NOS). These patterns could be accompanied by psychotic symptoms, rapid cycling, or other features. The severity can vary in different people, and it is not always the same person.

These are the major types of bipolar disorder.

Bipolar I. This type is diagnosed if the individual has at least one fully manic episode. No matter whether the individual has had past episodes, such as hypomania or clinical depressions, a full manic episode is enough to diagnose bipolar 1.

Bipolar II. When the individual has only experienced formal hypomanic episodes. An individual may have been depressed, but has not displayed full-blown manic episodes.

Cyclothymic Disorder is a form of hypomanic and mildly depressive symptoms. This disorder can last for up to two years. Although milder symptoms than bipolar I/II, cyclothymic syndrome can still cause difficulties and problems in everyday life. Cyclothymia is also known as bipolar disorder.

Bipolar disorderNOS - Bipolar disorderNOS refers only to episodes that do NOT last longer than the minimum number of symptoms. There is some debate as to whether certain temperaments should also be classified bipolar disorder noS. Some people may display temperaments that appear very similar to mild bipolar symptoms. These traits may then develop into more severe bipolar disorder.

Hyperthymic - Very happy, cheerful, extroverted and optimistic. Also, very confident.

Cyclothymic means fluctuating mild mood shifts, changing self-esteem

Dysthymic - Often joyless, low in energy, but not as severe depression.

Mixed depressive symptoms: mild symptoms of anxiety and sadness.

The Bipolar Spectrum is a classification of unipolar illnesses that may apply to individuals who have never had mania or hypomania. While bipolar disorder may be thought to be different from unipolar, there is no clear distinction. Bipolar disorder can manifest as a combination of symptoms that include depression and mild mood elevation. However, these symptoms are included in the bipolar spectrum. Individuals with these symptoms may be able to benefit from treatments commonly used for bipolar disorder. Some people who are diagnosed with unipolar depressive disorder develop hypomania as a result of starting antidepressant treatments. Although the boundaries are unclear and controversial, there is a possibility that half of all those who have been diagnosed with depression also suffer from bipolar disorder.

Individuals who fall into the bipolar spectrum are more likely to experience depression, marked fatigue, increased sleep quality, and feelings that feel like they're not sad.

Rapid Cycling: When you move from one episode, like depression, to another. DSM-IV says that rapid cycle is when a person has more than four episodes in a given year. However, it can be more common than that. Rapid cycling can sometimes occur within days or weeks. This condition is not uncommon and affects 15-25% of people suffering from bipolar disorder. People with rapid-cycling patterns have different treatment options than those without. Therefore, it is crucial that you know if your pattern is present. Rapid cycling people are more likely be females, younger age groups and to develop illnesses later in life. They may experience more hospitalizations and episodes. Rapid cycling can be caused by antidepressants or thyroid problems. For some, depression is their predominant experience.

Seasonal Patterns - Some people have episodes that occur at a particular time of year. You might find that it is more common to experience major depressive episodes in winter or autumn, and/or hypomanic or manic episodes during spring or summer. Recognizing these patterns may help you identify ways to decrease or eliminate the severity of your episode.

Signs & Symptoms

Bipolar disorder manifests as mood swings and mood fluctuations that can switch between depression or elevated mood. Bipolar disorder causes you to feel happy and energetic. You may also be impulsive or reckless. These manic episodes may cause you to feel sad, depressed and hopeless. Hypomania - a less severe type of mania - is generally characterized by feeling good and feeling more well-being.

Bipolar disorder does not mean that a person feels "down in his or her dumps," but they may also feel suicidal. These mood swings can be severe and more often occur than once a week. These mood swings do not have a definite pattern. One does not always occur before the other. It is also possible for mood swings to last for different periods of time. However, there are many treatments that can keep them under control and allow you to live a productive existence.

The average onset symptoms usually occurs at 25 years of age. Women and men are nearly equally affected by bipolar disorder. Bipolar Disorder I features at least one major depressive episode. These manic episodes can become so severe that they cause a loss of reality and significantly hinder daily functioning.

Bipolar I Disorders may necessitate a hospital stay.

Bipolar II Disorder sufferers might experience at best one major depression episode. These episodes may last from two to four weeks. At least one hypomanic episode may last at least four days. However, they are not subject to manic episodes. Cyclothymic disorder includes at least two consecutive years of hypomania and depression symptoms. These symptoms tend to be milder than major depressive episodes, hypomanic episodes, and hypomania. At least half of symptoms will be present during this time and may remain the same for up to two months. There are different stages of bipolar disorders. Signs and symptoms can vary greatly from one person or from one type to the other. These are the top signs and symptoms of bipolar disorder.

Manic Symptoms

DSM-5 describes a manic episode as an extreme and abnormal state or condition of severe, persistent, or prolonged irritable mood. A hypomanic episode on the other hand is one that lasts more than four days and is distinguished by a distinct and abnormal condition of severe, persistent, or extensive irritable mood.

If someone has been diagnosed as bipolar disorder, they may experience manic episodes.

A feeling of high energy, happiness, and elation for an extended time.

Restlessness

It is easy to get distracted

Feeling extremely annoyed

It's a race of thoughts through the mind

Jumping from one thought in one conversation

Talking very quickly

A lot of different projects to be taken on

Little sleep

Unlimited energy

Incredible confidence in your ability to do anything

Making impulsive or pleasurable high-risk purchases, poor financial investments, sexual indiscretions, and other such actions.

Increased agitation

High sex drive

Inflated self esteem

Feelings grandiosity

Increased goal-directed activity

Possible signs of detachment from reality include hallucinations or delusions

Making impossible plans and grand goals

Manic disorders can disrupt normal functioning at work, school, in relationships, and social situations. These behaviors do not occur due to a medical problem, alcohol or drug addiction, or side effects of a drug.

Depression symptoms

A major depressive episode can signify bipolar disorder's depressive side. This is when you feel depressed or lose interest in your life. These are some symptoms that may be experienced by people suffering from bipolar disorder.

For a majority of the day, feeling hopeless and sad.

Weight fluctuations – significant weight loss and weight gain

Affecting no enjoyment or interest in daily life

Indecisiveness

Sleep disturbances, such as oversleeping or insomnia

Heaviness or inertia

Inability of concentrating

Suicidal thoughts and/or attempts

Feeling guilty or worthless

Feelings and sensations of fatigue

Loss of Energy

Psychosis can also be described as a loss of connection to reality, delusions, or hallucinations.

Interest in activities that were once enjoyed is gone

Uncontrollable crying

Anxiety

The causes and risk factors

Bipolar disorder does not have a known cause. Researchers are still trying to determine the genetic causes and how the brain reacts to it. Researchers know of factors that increase your likelihood of developing the disorder. A family member who has the disorder increases the risk because of its highly inheritable nature.

While bipolar disorder is a genetic condition, some people are more susceptible than others to it. This means that even though some people may be predisposed to developing bipolar disorder, there are many factors such as psychological or environmental factors that can cause manic and depressive episodes. Not everyone will experience these episodes.

Family with the Disorder

A relative who has bipolar disorder within your family, such is a parent/sibling, can increase your chances of getting the disorder. Symptoms can first manifest as teenagers or early adults, with the average age at onset of the disorder being 25 years. Research revealed that children with severe mental illnesses had an average of a three-third chance to become mentally ill as adults. Researchers discovered that the risk of developing schizophrenia in children whose parents have been diagnosed early is higher if the parents are not diagnosed at an earlier age.

Genetics isn't the only factor. The genetics of bipolar disorder are highly heritable. However studies on identical twins showed that both will not develop it. It is possible for environmental factors to play a role in increasing the risk or decreasing it.

High stress

People who are exposed to trauma have a greater chance of developing bipolar disorder. An increase in the risk of developing the disorder later on in life may be due to childhood traumas like abuse or neglect, loss of parents, or any other traumatic events. Extremely stressful events, like the loss of a job, moving to a different environment or a death in a family, can also lead to manic or depressive episodes. Also, a manic episode could be caused by insufficient sleep.

Substance Abuse

A bipolar disorder can also develop from the abuse of drugs and alcohol. While the substance itself doesn't cause the disorder directly, it can trigger mood episodes or accelerate its onset. A manic or depressive episode can also be caused by medications. A doctor may ask you to stop using substances to diagnose bipolar disorder. Substance abuse can also trigger psychosis.

Brain Structure

Two types of brain scans are available: functional magnetic resonance image (fMRI) or positron emissions technology (PET). While certain findings from brain scans could be linked to bipolar disorders, further research is needed to determine the exact impact of these findings on bipolar disorder and how it affects treatment and diagnosis.

Gender

Bipolar disorder affects both men & women equally. But, while women are at greater risk of experiencing mood swings that can be rapid and severe, they are also more vulnerable to it. Women are more at risk for experiencing depressive and mixed episodes than men. Here are some questions you can ask to determine whether you are at increased risk for bipolar disorders:

Is your family affected by bipolar disorder and other mental disorders?

Has your family ever been through trauma?

Recent stress events or sleep deprivation?

Are there any drastic changes in your mood following the use of drugs or alcohol

These mood swings can have a negative impact on your relationships, work, or daily activities.

Even if you don't know the answer, you can still discuss your concerns with your doctor to receive a diagnosis. If you are already suffering from the disorder and you are concerned about the health of your children, it is worth speaking to a professional to discuss the options that may be available to you to ensure their mental wellbeing.

Realizing Your Goal

Once you have successfully divided the goals into steps then you can start planning the implementation of the progress and evaluating it. If you need help with problem solving or changing the timeframe, it might be worth considering dividing the goal into smaller steps. Sometimes, it may be necessary to give up on a goal you care about. It is important to remember that alternative goals can be found by considering your capabilities and values. This will help you to identify realistic goals that match your goals. This will allow you to continue doing the important things that are important to you.

Find Something You Love

Your life will be more meaningful and fulfilling if you find something you enjoy. There are many activities that will enrich your life, including playing with your pet, walking with a friend, and supporting a cause that you believe in. Our lives are all different. You need to find the things that make you happy.

Get rid of junk food.

It may be tempting to eat a burger, fry, or chips in order to distract from feelings of loneliness. However, this will only make your depression worse. If you are feeling down, it is important that you eat healthy meals.

A meal plan is important.

Bipolar disorder patients need to be able to keep their rhythm. Regular meals are important for bipolar disorder patients. Eat your meals and snacks on a regular basis. This will keep your body active, sugar levels stable, mood stable, and energy high. This habit will prevent you from snacking too often. You must not skip a meal.

Be kind to you.

Most bipolar medications can cause weight gain. This could negatively affect your self esteem. You might feel annoyed, upset, or embarrassed by your appearance. This could lead to depression. You should be compassionate with yourself, and don't become depressed if this happens. Talk to your doctor if weight loss is something you want. Do not resort to fad weight loss.

A few simple changes to your eating habits can help you feel better and less depressed.

Chapter 12: 17 Ways To Naturally Overcome Bipolar Disorder Using No Medication

Nothing beats regular exercise

Enjoy some exercise, running in the park, going swimming or just walking. Regular exercise can relieve stress. It will allow you to breathe easier and help you get rid of any thoughts or worries. You can improve your brain chemistry by doing it at least 30 times per day.

Exercise can help increase blood flow, boost self-esteem, and pump more blood to the veins. It has been proven that exercise can help overcome depression and bipolar disorder.

Are you in a bad mood today? You don't have to be discouraged from going outside. You can get some fresh air and lift your spirits. Take a break and keep moving forward.

Good Nights of Sleep

Lack of sleep can cause problems in every system of the body. People with mental illness will have difficulty thinking straight or clear. Manic episodes can result from too much or too little sleep. This is why it is so important to maintain a good sleep schedule. To go to sleep at 10 in the night and get up at 6 in morning, It shouldn't matter what time a person puts in to going to bed at night and waking up at dawn, it should be an established routine. Who knows? He may suddenly be in a better state simply because he gets regular sleep.

Choose the Right Diet

You are a certified coffee lover Are you a certified coffee lover? A healthy diet and proper nutrition can help prevent certain symptoms. Decaffeinated, as well caffeinated, coffee should be dropped from this list. Why? It is because it helps stabilize mood swings.

Skipping meals is not an option. You should also avoid eating unhealthy snacks. Instead, eat whole grains like brown rice, wheatbread, oatmeal and whole grain cereals.

Turn off the TV

Believe it or not, TV viewing is an unnatural way for one to increase their mental strength. People suffering from bipolar disorder need to avoid watching videos and even playing video games. It will only cause excessive excitement or depression. Rapidly changing TV programs and commercials can have a negative impact on the brain's chemical imbalance. It is important to avoid the television in order to restore mental health and get one's life on track.

Read Decent Books

Reading books of interest, especially ones that contain positive content, helps to strengthen and slow down your mind. It stimulates creativity and mental effort. Because silence reading can be quietening and calms the minds, people with mental disorders often choose to read as their form for recreation.

Get some Magazines and Newspapers in your Hands

It can be very depressing to watch news programs on TV. This form of media has a significant impact on your mental health. It's better not to read any magazines or newspapers to keep abreast of current events. Reading is gentler on your mind and can strengthen it. Reading is also more flexible than watching television.

Never Believe in the Occult of the Supernatural.

Avoiding things that seem unreal or can only be troublesome to the mind is best. These things may be seen in movies, or at certain events. You should avoid these items as they can cause a negative effect, especially for those who are addicted to them.

The Five Senses

You can listen to soothing music. Take a moment to smell the fragrant flowers in the garden. Enjoy a bowl with ice cream. View a feel good program. You can take a refreshing hot shower.

Positive mood can be achieved by using the senses. This will help you feel more at ease, and it will prevent mood swings.

Establish a Support Base

This saying is very true. It is possible to release the whole burden of his thoughts by having a supportive network with people who are easy to talk to. This will help him feel calmer and more relaxed. He doesn't have the ability to solve his problems on his own. Other people can help him stay on top of things.

Face Your Fears

Sometimes, it can be scary to confront your fear. It can be hard to get the courage you need. You may already feel anxious or helpless as a result of these fears. These factors can also increase stress. Being patient and learning to overcome your fears can be liberating.

Be open for communication

Is it okay to talk to someone about issues from the past? There's no reason to be embarrassed. It is essential to openly discuss any past or present issues with family, friends or professionals. People with mental disorders may find stability if they can let go of any problems.

Don't allow others to define you

"You are sick." "You have bipolar disorder." Rejecting any kind of label will only discourage someone who is trying to get better. The more one attempts to clear his mind of the flood, the worse it will get.

Recovering from a mental illness is not possible if one admits to the faults of others. The process of restoring mental balance can take time. But, it is possible to learn strategies to heal both the mind & body.

A Coach Can Help

A coach who focuses on mental health is an ideal option for those who are experiencing mental health difficulties. It is much less expensive than therapy and works well when used in conjunction with therapy.

Life coaches who focus on bipolar disorder may not be easy to find, but someone who has experience with ADHD might be. There are things that both conditions can benefit from.

Medications can cause problems

It is dangerous to stop taking medications when symptoms appear. The person taking medication should not be able to stop taking them quickly. It's a great idea to speak with your doctor about quitting medication, especially when it's not helping with your mental health.

Never Lose Hope

Do you feel that things are a bit slow lately? You wonder if you can still make things work? It's certain that time heals. Don't let this discourage you and never lose hope. There's always another day and there's no need to remain stuck in the same situation forever. Be patient and there will be better days.

Things do not happen overnight

There is no quick way to overcome depression or bipolar disorder. It takes effort, determination, patience, perseverance, and lots of hard work. Never give up and don't ever stop working towards your goals. Everyone deserves to live the life of their dreams.

Just as others say, "It's all in the head." You don't need to immediately take any drugs or medication to solve your problems. People suffering from bipolar disorder must be positive. Keep your positive outlook on life even when it's not working out.

It is essential to live a happy, healthy life. It's always safer to do things the best way possible.

Chapter 13: What Is Depression And What Causes It?

Depression (MDD), a severe form of depression, is the most painful type of pain one could ever experience. It's considered unbearable for many. Suicide is the leading reason for death. The suicide of a loved one is a leading cause of death worldwide.

Depression takes away the ability to study and work, as well as maintain healthy relationships. It also makes it difficult for us to have fun with our favorite activities. Many believe depression to be a moral problem.

We can beat depression. There are evidence-based and affordable ways to overcome depression. There are many alternative therapies that have been scientifically evaluated and approved. It is possible to make changes in your lifestyle and the environment you live in. These include exercising and healthy eating.

Scientifically, it is also proven that spiritual and religious-based activities are beneficial in helping depressed individuals. These strategies combined can improve your chances of beating the depression.

Depression is real. Many people do not believe it to be a medical issue. Many people only believe in it when they or a family member are affected by this disease. Or, it may be too late (suicide).

The so-called complementary tests, laboratory tests, and imaging are all useful tools in medicine. Biomarkers are used to confirm the presence of disease. There aren't any biological markers to diagnose psychiatric conditions (1). The clinical examination determines the diagnosis.

This information allows us to see that in the absence of any evidence (biological marks), depression is not conclusive. Depression is a well-known mental disorder. Apathy, sadness, and loss in interest or pleasure are the core symptoms. Secondary symptoms can include feelings such as guilt, low self-esteem or low self confidence, changes in sleep quality, length, appetite, bodyweight, and excessive fatigue.

Depression has almost no cause. Sometimes, however, depression can be triggered by either small or major factors. Depression can occur suddenly and it can also start slowly. It can also occur suddenly. It can last several months, years or even a lifetime. The degree of unhappiness is increasing day by day. There is less interest or pleasure in some things than others. A global emptiness overtakes.

We should not ignore MDD. It's the same thing as allowing the enemy control us without fighting. This is not a tragedy that should happen to you, your loved one, or a stranger. Please be kind! It is important to know the difference between MDD (malaise) and sadness.

Anxiety can lead to sadness such as loss of a close friend, financial troubles, joblessness, or other negative events. Sadness can be an unpleasant feeling. Some define it as emotional distress. Others describe it with chest tightness or emotional distress.

Sadness signals that something's wrong. It is not something we want. Most of us will feel this at some time in our lives. To be honest, we feel it all the time. Sadness can be a normal, desirable and even pleasant feeling, even though it can be quite debilitating (2). Depression can cause depression to be severe in its severity, duration, and damages. Depression doesn't benefit anyone who is suffering beyond what they expect and something that is different from normal sadness.

Normal grief encourages people to fight despite their pain. Depression is a condition that leaves us with no choice but to give up and go home. The former leaves you with the urge to fight. The latter puts us in a bind. It causes disability and suffering that goes beyond normal sadness. There is urgent need for compassion and assistance for those who are suffering from depression.

Even though we are getting enough sleep, excessive fatigue is common. Then there's insomnia, when you can't fall asleep. It is almost a form of martyrdom, as the sleepless nights do not seem to end. We gradually lose appetite and our body weight. Some dishes we used to enjoy are no more appealing. On the other side, our appetites and body mass can rise. Because of a distorted body, self-esteem is affected.

We cut ourselves off from the people we care about. We don't like to answer the phones. We feel terrible, stupid, or even naive. We lose the ability of feeling pleasure and interest in activities that were once enjoyable, like studying, working, maintaining relationships or exercising.

The ability to do what you used to do is gone. We don't perform the same as before the depression. We feel completely helpless and ineffective. We believe that our intelligence and attention, memory, and all that makes up human nature, will disappear. We believe we are despicable.

Depression can last for several days, weeks or even years. It may be due to one or more causes, whether they are big or small. It could seem inexplicable. It can be mildly, moderately, or severely. It can ultimately drain our precious, vital life fuel: hope. Then depression can strike, leading to suicide attempts or making it impossible for us to live a normal life.

This is why students often miss classes and fail to complete work. It can disrupt interpersonal relationships. It can lead people to drink and use illicit drugs. It can cause pre-existing problems. It can also lead to suicide as an extreme act desperation.

The Diagnostic and Statistical Manual of Mental Disorders (5th edition). American Psychiatric Association (2013 Edition) states that a person must experience depression for at minimum two weeks to be classified as a depressive episode. The person will feel sadness or a loss of interest or pleasure or both. Children and adolescents may feel angry, rather than sad (3).

According to current classifications, the main symptoms are sadness and/or loss in interest/pleasure. Additional symptoms can also occur (3).

Changes in appetite, body weight, or both in the last month of the previous month that are at least 5%

Sleeping too much or insomnia

Psychomotor agitation/retardement

Feelings that you are not worthy, devalued or have low self-esteem, such as guilt and shame.

Fatigue, or loss of energy

Inattention, indecision

Suicidal thoughts, or thoughts about dying

Some symptoms can result in significant disability and suffering in family, personal, and social relations, school performance, and work. It could be in any of these areas, or it can occur in all three.

Depression does not usually have a cause. Although there is usually a triggering issue, depression symptoms often persist regardless of whether the problem has resolved. After three months, 2 out 5 people with depression get better. A quarter of depressed people get better within the first 12 months.

Cultural background affects how a person feels and reports symptoms. This, in turn, influences the diagnosis. Some patients may state, "I feel sad." Others will say that they are a nervous wreck. Others have vague physical symptoms. Nearly 70% of people suffering from depression only report somatic symptoms (physical). Depression is often not diagnosed or suspected. The patient cannot refer to somatic complaints. These are mostly subjective such as in the head or stomach.

It is possible for children or adolescents to behave rebelliously. Do not let your guard down! These patients suffer more than adults simply because they don't know what to say. Elderly can remain silent about their depression. They might complain only of physical problems. Please do not confuse them with the common complaints that elderly people have.

You will need to have a medical evaluation to determine if they are healthy. The suffering must be felt and the losses must be compensated for. This is not just a list (3). It is essential to perform a thorough diagnosis. It will establish the best treatment plan for each case. It is enough to have normal sadness. It is not necessary to receive specialized treatment. There are treatments for depression and they must be performed only by licensed professionals.

100% of the diagnosis in Psychiatry can be made clinically. The history taking and the physical, mental, and psychological examination of the patient will help us determine what the problem is. Sometimes, however, laboratory tests may be required. Other medical problems may require Computed Tomography, (CT) scans, or Magnetic Resonance Imaging. For monitoring if the medication is altering other physiological functions or not, there are many tests that can be done. The initial tests serve to provide baseline information for future treatment.

MDD is believed to be caused in part by an interaction of genetic and environmental risk factors (5-9). This is the exact same as in diabetes and cardiovascular issues, which are multifactorial. Environment hazards include prenatal problems such as emotional loss, deprivations and suffering, stress (5-9), wars (5-9), insufficient social support, inadequate food and exercise.

Possible connections between MDD, drug use (licit and illegal) and other medical conditions is also possible.

Conclusion: Depression is multifactorial. It involves genetic inheritance and complex interactions with the environment. A person who has had a family history with depression or other mood disorders is more likely to be depressed. But, this does NOT mean that the person will always develop this illness. This knowledge is vital because it allows you to take actions on the factors that facilitate depression. MDD can either be avoided or at least reduced.

Some aspects encourage depression to occur. These enablers are often called risk factors. MDD may not be caused by all of these risk factors. However the likelihood that MDD will occur is greater if they are present. They must be prevented or reduced as soon as possible. Sometimes, there's nothing we can do.

A person who is highly anxious (neurotic), or overly worried about most things.

Stressful situations or situations that are standard for others can easily trigger depression. Psychotherapy helps the patient with nervousness to develop skills to deal with problems and prevent depression from triggering.

Traumatic events include violence in childhood. It is possible to help with surveillance and prevention.

Genetic inheritance. Two to four times as likely to be depressed than are their first-degree relatives. It is important to treat depression as soon as it appears.

Other psychiatric disorders, such as anxiety and attention deficit-hyperactivity disorder (ADHD). These disorders are best treated promptly to avoid depression or reduce its incidence.

Other medical issues, such as diabetes and cardiovascular disease. MDD can also be prevented by proper treatment.

Chapter 14: Include Your Environment

This exercise demands that you be strong of your mind and will. Even the most strong people sometimes need to look around for support and guidance. This is one the most significant contributing factors. Here are some more issues you need to consider:

1) Talk with people

Start with your immediate relatives and children. Do not close off the lines. Explain to them exactly what is happening. People criticize because people don't know. If they know they will help you in whatever way they can.

Problems and family relationships can be very stressful, especially if you are married or have children. Your children and your partner won't understand you if you don't explain it to them. Their behavior towards you will increase stress. This is exactly what you do not want or need.

You shouldn't be ashamed to invite co-workers, business partners and other employees into the vault. You never know who might be suffering from the same condition. It's possible to create a group therapy program and support one another. Even if none of them suffer from the same condition, they will try to alleviate your stress by not judging you.

2) Seek support

If you feel like you need more support that your family members and friends can offer, it is worth looking into specialized organizations that have the ability to give you what you need professionally and correctly.

Balance your social life

People with bipolar disorder are more likely to isolate or overstimulate themselves. This can ruin relationships and break up friendships. Try to find some balance by taking up a hobby or doing volunteer work in something that interests you. This will take your mind off of the problem and help you act normally.

Because mathematics was included in the process, let us see the correct equation.

Natural products + lifestyle, psychology + environment = Overcoming BPD

Chapter 15: The Bipolar Diet

They say that your food is what makes you feel good. You can have a negative effect on your mood by what you eat. Eat healthy foods to manage your bipolar symptoms. You need to lead a healthy lifestyle.

Avoid certain foods

It is important to avoid foods that trigger manic or depressive symptoms.

1. Caffeine

Caffeine works as a stimulant. Caffeine is a stimulant. It can cause both depression and mania. It can also interfere with your sleep. Your caffeine intake is a key factor in managing your bipolar disorder.

Caffeine consumption increases anxiety, irritability, and hyperactivity. It also causes racing and disturbs thoughts.

2. Alcohol

Reduce alcohol intake for bipolar disorder. Your mood may be affected by alcohol.

3. Sugar

Consuming a high-sugar diet may make it harder to lose weight. Bipolar treatment could be affected by obesity. It can also lead to mood disorders. Sugar intake can also be a factor in bipolar disorder.

4. Salt

Salt intake is difficult and can negatively impact your lithium levels. Reduce salt intake to manage bipolar symptoms.

5. Fat

It is possible to control your bipolar disorder by decreasing your trans fats intake and increasing your saturated fat intake. This means that low-fat dairy products should be used and lean protein should be preferred.

Avoid these foods if your anti-depressant medication is in effect.

Champagne

Bananas

Liver

Fermented Cheese

Chianti

Soya Sauce

Grapefruit juice

These foods can cause drug interactions that could be dangerous with your medications.

Foods to Try

There are many food items that positively affect your mood.

Berries

Different types, including blueberries, raspberries, and strawberries, all contain Vitamin C. Antioxidants help regulate the production cortisol. Eating berries can help stabilize your blood pressure. It will also lower your heart beat. It will also relieve depression symptoms.

Whole grains

Whole grains are healthier options to high-fat foods such as white bread, white pasta, and white rice. These amazing super foods also have a calm effect on your mind. It can increase serotonin production in your brain. This can help to ease symptoms of anxiety or depression.

Fish

If you're suffering from manic episodes, you can indulge in fatty fish. Omega-3 fatty acids are found in many fishes, including tuna salmon, salmon, mackerel sardines and halibut. These foods provide relief from depression and manic episodes.

Dairy products

Cheese and yogurt are rich in riboflavin, which helps calm your nerves. This is a great time to add these nutritious foods to your grocery cart.

Bananas & Oranges - and Apples

These three extraordinary fruits can make a huge difference in your body's health. These fruits are rich sources of vitamin C as well as fiber, which is essential for improving your immune function.

Herbal Tea

Drinking herbal teas like chamomile or lavender can help calm you during manic episodes.

Magnesium-rich foods

Magnesium, which has the same effect that lithium, is often used to calm moods. Magnesium can reduce the symptoms associated with rapid cycling or mania by being added to your daily routine. Magnesium reduces manic episodes including insomnia. These are some excellent sources:

Avocado - Avocado is an amazing superfood, loaded with multivitamins. One half avocado can help you manage the symptoms of bipolar disorder.

Bananas, - Bananas have a high potassium content. Bananas are high in vitamin C, fiber, and magene.

Fish - Fish are rich in vitamin D and omega-3 oils.

Soybeans, - Soybeans have high fiber, minerals. Black beans, white bean, kidney beans chickpeas lentils and black-eyed Peas.

Low-fat yogurt -- This delicious, healthy snack contains high levels of calcium and magnesium.

Nuts/seeds: Nuts and seed such as Brazil nuts or cashews have high magnesium levels. These nuts help to keep your hunger levels down and your energy levels up.

8. Nutrient-rich food products

People with bipolar disorder often have vitamin deficiencies. Here are the foods that should be included in your daily diet

Vitamin D

Vitamin D is essential for mood stabilization. You should eat plenty of vitamin D-rich foods like cod liver oil.

Vitamin C

Vitamin C-rich foods can include yellow bell Peppers, guavas and kale as well kiwi fruit and broccoli.

Vitamin B

Thiamin-rich foods such as whole-grain and whole cereal cereals as well as baked goods and dark green leafy vegetable should be eaten.

Bipolar Rules for Eating

In order to eat food that will improve your mood, here are some rules:

It's possible to make eating an art.

How you feel is shown by how you eat. Are you feeling distracted, frustrated, or fast? Your attitude towards food can impact how you react to it. Many experts agree that the way you eat impacts how you feel. Make eating a art to improve your mood. You must eat mindfully.

Avoid eating in front a TV. Be mindful of what you are eating before you order. Make sure to appreciate the food's textures and colors. After you've finished eating, take some time to appreciate the flavors. Do you like the taste of your food? Is it spicy or sweet? What are its ingredients? Take your time when eating and taking the time to chew it. This mindfulness exercise has been shown effective in reducing the symptoms of depression or bipolar.

It is important that you take your medication carefully.

It is essential to take your medication seriously. Talk to your doctor about your medications before you start taking them.

Is it okay for me to take my medication on an empty stomach. Do you think grapefruit juice is safe to consume while taking your medication. You should be aware that certain foods may cause drug interactions. It is dangerous to consume alcohol if you take psychotropic drugs. Take care to not ingest too much sodium when taking lithium.

Keep a food journal.

Do you eat virtually nothing during your manic episodes. Do you regularly eat more than four bags of chips when feeling depressed? It is known that the foods you eat greatly affect your mood. Therefore, it is important to keep a food diary. Every day, write down all the food you eat. A food log will help you understand your eating habits. This will make it much easier for you to correct your eating patterns.

Get rid of junk food.

It may be tempting to eat burgers, fried foods, and chips, but this will only distract you from the loneliness that can lead to depression. If you are feeling down, it is important that you eat healthy meals.

A meal plan is important.

People with bipolar disorder believe rhythm is the king. Regular meals are important for bipolar disorder patients. Eat your meals and snacks on a regular basis. This will keep you feeling energized and stable in sugar levels, as well. This habit will help you avoid snacking too often. It is important to not skip a meal.

Be kind to you.

Most bipolar medications can cause weight gain. This could have a significant impact on your self-esteem. You may feel annoyed, upset, or even embarrassed about how you look. This could lead to depression. You should be compassionate with yourself, and don't become depressed if this happens. Talk to your doctor if weight loss is something you want. Avoid trying to lose your weight by following fad or trendy diets.

A few lifestyle changes can help to stabilize your mood, and alleviate depression symptoms.

Chapter 16: Nutritional And Diet

Treatment of children with bipolar disorder is based on nutrition and diet. Bipolar disorder can result in food cravings and poor eating habits. Food cravings, overeating, and weight gain can all lead to bipolar disorder. Different foods may affect the symptoms of bipolar disorder in children.

There are two main food issues common to bipolar kids: constipation or weight gain. Be sure to feed your child high-fiber fruits, vegetables, fruits, along with plenty of water. Replace high-sugar and sugary drinks with water and low-calorie options such as fruit juices or water. You can prevent weight gain by eating fruits, vegetables, and low-carb snacks.

The bipolar diet should, at a minimum consist of:

Very few refined carbs

There is limited sugar

Limited caffeine

Healthy food at regular, scheduled times

Bipolar Diet Special Issues

Sugar and Carb Cravings

Bipolar kids often crave unhealthy foods like empty calories and saturated fats. Bipolar children may feel more mood swings if they have a craving for sugar and carbs. Bipolar kids have a unique brain chemistry which causes them to crave sugar and carbs. Your child may crave high fructose or caffeine-rich beverages that are intensely stimulatory. This can lead to more severe symptoms.

Sometimes, eating these types foods can cause a decrease in appetite. In this case, your child may not be able to eat the regular healthy meals necessary for good health. Poor eating habits can make your child more moody and could even lead to bipolar disorder. In addition to binging on sweets and carb-rich meals, your child might also become overheated or display signs of binging. A change in the pattern and frequency of your appetite can be a sign of depression or stress. As a parent you can limit the intake of sugar-rich foods and carbs that your child consumes.

Omega 3

In 1999, Dr. Andrew Stoll published a study showing that omega-3 fatty oils could improve bipolar disorder. Human brains require omega 3s for proper functioning. Omega - 3 helps regulate mood and keeps brain membranes fluid. The consumption of omega 3s has decreased in recent years. This is because we eat less omega 3-rich fish and more hydrogenated oil. Omega 3s are found on oily fish, green veggies, walnuts, flaxseed, and flaxseed.

LNA, EPA, & DHA are all three types of omega 3 fatty acids which are essential in mood regulation. Research shows that these three omega-3 fatty acids work in a similar way as anticonvulsants or lithium. Biederman found that omega 3s have been shown to improve some children's mania. The FDA has approved that 3 grams daily of omega 3 (fish Oil) is safe for both children as well as adults.

Vitamins und minerals

Many feel the need to find natural alternatives for children due to side effects from mood stabilizers.

Neurotransmitters

Neurotransmitters, including serotonin (dopamine), serotonin (serotonin), and norepinephrine (norepinephrine), are essential for basic functions of the body, such as motor skills. Neurotransmitters, which are vitamins, minerals and essential amino acids, are produced by the brain. Natural options can also affect the levels of neurotransmitters, just as prescription bipolar medications. Studies done on adult bipolar patients showed that having enough serotonin in your body can cause symptoms like depression and manic mania. You can boost your serotonin levels by eating salmon, turkeys, eggs cheese, pineapples, tofu and nuts.

B Vitamins and Folic acid

Vitamin B12 as well as folic acid have been a subject of interest in research to find natural treatment for bipolar disorder. Both are essential for the production of neurotransmitters. Deficiency in any of them can lead patients to experience depressive symptoms. Vitamin B12 can also be found in enriched soy or ricemilk, fortified breakfast foods, meat, poultry, eggs, milk and dairy. Folic Acids are abundant in citrus fruits, avocado, broccoli, and dark leafy leaves.

The suprachiasmatic Nucleus and Melatonin

The suprachiasmatic nocleus (or SCN) regulates hormones that regulate human alertness. SCN also controls melanin. Research has shown that bipolar children make different amounts of melanin at various times. Many children with bipolar disorder have a reverse-sleep-wake cycle. Melatonin is made in the body from fruits, vegetables (vegetables), nuts, and seeds.

Chapter 17: Are There Movies That Accurately Portray Someone With Borderline Personality Disorder (Bpd)?

There are many wonderful movies out that capture the essence BPD. But they do so from the perspective a person affected by pwBPD. Eternal Sunshine of the Spotless Mind), etc.) and/or diluting the subject material in the fiction/storyline. Anna Karenina). This video is an inside look at BPD and does a wonderful job. This movie is a must-see if it has not been seen. David Lynch may love to direct female characters with BPD. But his previous attempts (e.g. Twin Peaks: Fire Walk with Me: Laura Palmer (Lynch) isn't as smooth and polished as his character in this movie, which was brilliantly played by Naomi Watts. This is the best acting I've ever seen. The movie is so great that it can save you from reading boring, difficult, long books.

A few warnings, though (hopefully not with spoilers)

This movie is scary and dark. The film depicts a person with severe BPD. She is not receiving treatment. It's hard to watch. This film shows the worst parts of BPD through BPD sufferer's eyes. In the movie, she does something truly horrible. This is because most pwBPD do not suffer from this level of emotional turmoil.

Another problem is that the storyline is quite complicated, which is common with David Lynch movies. This means that many people don't understand the movie and become confused afterward. This is partially due to the complicated plot but also because most people are completely ignorant about BPD. This is a complex topic that requires knowledge. David Lynch's "BPD for Dummies" manual is lacking. There are no specific explanations provided in the movie. You also do not get a DSM-5 excerpt with your Cinema ticket, DVD, or Netflix subscription. It is an "insider film". The movie is best viewed if you already have a good understanding of BPD.

What is it like for someone with borderline personality dysfunction to be loved?

I believe you'll find many here had experience with a untreated partner who deceived their BPD diagnosis. This is a disaster scenario in the worst case.

Everything that you believe your partner says during the initial stages of the relationship's idealization phase is false. Every love phrase you hear in your direction is not true. This is because it is part of a mirroring scheme, which will be denied later.

Even if words are written in great detail they can be forgotten later. You are described by many as the long-awaited soulmate. The discovered treasure. The partner they long for. All their love, all words, all plans, any promises, and all commitments will be disregarded later on as that untreated partner invariably cycles into the "devalue" stage and starts to burn the house down.

With someone who isn't 100%, you are in a hall with mirrors. Most people are unable to comprehend what is about to unfold in front of them when they first encounter BPD.

Words that are used in normal relationships do not mean anything to a partner with BPD. Don't believe a word that they say. As they cycle you will be bombarded by upside down gaslighting. Once you have found the lost treasure, you will be the one suffering from BPD. You are clearly a demon deceiver that deserves to be punished.

Once you know what is happening, it is very easy to decide. Your partner untreated in the early stages will mirror you. In the later stages, the reverse is true. They will project their illness onto others.

129

This is a very small glimpse into the psycho halls full of mirrors you will be experiencing.

Staying puts your mental health in danger. You will not make it through the BPD shitstorm, which is headed in your direction.

If your partner refuses a diagnosis and does not want to be treated for ongoing BPD (not general therapy), you need to get out. Deceptions can continue without treatment. It will only continue to get worse.

DO NOT MAKE ANY FINANCIAL ADVESTMENTS OR COMMITMENTS TO THAT DIRECTION. It will not be tolerated.

All personal information you share with others should be kept secret. In the final smear campaign against you, anything shared with untreated partners can be used against them. It could take weeks or even years.

It is important to understand that your partner will not treat you well. There are other options. Make the best of it while you have mental health.

What is the worst about having borderline personality disorders?

It's not a problem that I have to deal with every day. The worst part of it all would be when I find someone who I like enough that I want to idolize. That kind of takes it all out for me.

The person makes me dependent, even though I don't normally interact with anyone beyond a superficial level. This person suddenly appears to be the whole of existence. They are everything. That makes most people uncomfortable. It can be uncomfortable, especially if it is so far from my normal self. I'm quite a different person as that. It's also not one that's highly sought-after.

It's like a secret 2 year old within me emerges and becomes very apparent. I have become a person I want to spend time with. As a toddler, my needs are constant.

Then I begin to hate my self because I don't love that two-year-old, and I don't wish to remember her existence. I do not want her to be seen by anyone else. She is weak. It pains me to even think about it, let alone write about it.

Usually, the other person starts to hate me. Or maybe it's all in my head. I act as if they can't take it, even though I'm sure I can't. How could anyone else? Maybe they ruin it. But then the other person leaves. I suspect it scares them.

That's when devaluing gets started. They saw the poor two-year-old, and were disgusted. So they left. I don't like it, too. But I can't keep it from my mind. This frustrates me. I hate my self for having her in myself, for letting people know about her, and I hate them more for being afraid and leaving me to figure how to lock it up.

And then, I try and kill myself. Every time. Maybe I'm just trying to get rid my two-year old even though it means I have to give the rest away with it.

I try not be idealistic. It happens very rarely. It always ends badly. It's the worst part of BPD.

What is it really like to be friends or family with someone with borderline personality disorder

My opinion does not always fit into the same mold of other BPDs.

It's not always enjoyable. It's an emotional rollercoaster with NOS, which has turns at g powers that would rip your face. Lows so low, they'd send you to Mordor in five weeks. Includes all meals, bar, and tips

It is a constant. How is it possible that you have stopped using Facebook? Did you block me? I was blocked by you?

It's not simple. Sometimes it can be great. Sometimes it's lonely. I have three or four people who text me every couple months to make sure that I am still breathing. We'll send a snapchat. Maybe a SMS. I will abruptly stop. That will be it for the next few months. The cycle continues. I never answer the phone. I hate telephone calls. But it's not constant. Never steady. I'm not reliable. It's not when I'm "in a phase". I am always funny and am in good spirits when I am not in a "... "phase". Come on over for drinks...let's go out to the club! But I could get jealous..and then my panic will set in...and then it's over! It's a shitshow!

There are times when I am lucid, and I control my actions for the most parts. I can socially interact with people quite well. I would be unaware that I am "damaged products". I love to go to car shows in my 2010 Camaro 2SS. It's a great way for me to meet other car lovers and even help a grease monkey tighten up a few clamps.

I'll host a game of Cards Against Humanity in my home with my husband's coworkers as well as their wives. Make sure everyone is fed and served drinks. I make baby rugs for all the women in their lives at my husband's local Sheriff's Department.

During bad times, I delete my social media. Because I believe someone is mad, or being mean to me, when they most likely aren't. It's the old "making a mountain from a molehill" saying. I won't see it any other way, and I am convinced of that. Sometimes I will block people or unfriend them. They won't be able to tell. It's how I've lost so many close friends. This has also happened to my family members.

It is lonely sometimes, because it is always revolving...it is always changing. However, most people are unable to endure the ups & downs it brings. The ups or downs that it brings. I only do it for me.

Is it possible that a person with borderline personality dysfunction can change?

Yes.

It is hard to forget the stigma that surrounds the disorder.

The definition of "BPD" will depend on the person who it is, but Marsha Linhan has described BPD as something that can easily evolve into "BPD+". With the right self-compassion, anyone with BPD may experience remarkable changes.

I could have never imagined the feelings that I have today two or three years ago. I don't mean to spoil it, but our empathy paradigm contains hidden talents...

Yeah. Facilitation, yo! DBT didn't fix everything, but it got me on track with the right principles.

It is rare that I'm not thankful for my life. Of course, results vary. DBT isn't always available to everyone. However, it can be done. I'm referring to the fact that we can change our affects quite often when compared with neurotypical individuals, and this is a major part of dysregulation.

...but I suspect you're referring to treatment rather than symptomicity.

Sometimes change can seem messy. Therapy therapy is meant to help you with your brain, relationships with others, and even the most abstract concept of 'personality '....

...but we can change fairly frequently, I don't think so. It's all well!

This should be helpful. :)

Do borderline personality disorder patients have to give up on their partners?

BPD is something I have personally experienced.

BPD sufferers find it difficult to keep a person in their mind as a whole. When someone does something to them that triggers them, they often forget all the good things about that person and will see them as bad.

BPD is when a person feels abandoned, rejected, criticized, etc. They will usually act out on that pain because it is something they don't want to feel. But they don't know the rationale for doing so. You can discuss things or come up with a mutually-beneficial solution. cooperation. They do not have other defense mechanisms.

If someone with BPD realizes that they have acted too recklessly after the discard, it might be too painful. In this case, they might choose to believe that they truly hate you. This is because it's less shameful than feeling ashamed of having acted so outrageously.

They might not even realize they did it and feel tremendous regret. But they do really hate themselves. Believe that. It's not uncommon to feel like the trash of the earth. It's not the apology that they wish to avoid, but it's the shame associated with it.

Sometimes they may dissociate and not feel anything after an outburst. They don't want regret, shame, or any other feelings, so they just go completely numb.

BPD sufferers can misunderstand the initial event that caused them to have a bad relationship. They may also see it as an act of abandonment, rejection, or attack. Misinterpretation can still happen. BPD sufferers often carry too much baggage in order to'stop pain'. It is because they have many templates in their brains. Short-circuits exist to protect them. If person A does thing B and says thing C then it must mean D and they must be stopped/discarded/ignored/hurt by revenge/etc. They fail in reality testing and come up with no realistic alternatives.

Chapter 18: Effects Of Borderline Policy Disorder Sur Family And Relationship

It can be very difficult to deal with an adult child, parent or sibling, a spouse, friend, relative, or colleague with BPD. This puts a lot on all relationships as well as all family members. BPD sufferers tend to be very self-involved because of their neurobiological shortcomings. However, they don't understand how difficult it can be for you and your family to help. Sometimes, they view your suggestions as power and ignore them. In the end, you feel upset, confused, unsure and sick. BPD can sometimes seem like a oneway street. Jessica, a TARA participant, heard the stories from other members of the group and began to ask, "You don't even know?" It doesn't add up! "You don't count!" Family members feel ignored, dismissed, mocked, and left unrealized in an invalidating atmosphere.

Families are often in an infirmating environment, where love and concern is ignored, distrusted, and even attacked. BPD influences every relationship differently and each partner has different expectations. Your relationship with the BPD individual will have an impact on the consistency and nature of your relationship. It also depends on the amount of support and understanding you provide.

Parents of Bipolar Personality Disorder patients (BPD)

The attitude and way that parents treat their BPD children reflects how they approach all aspects of their life. The other parent could be permissive, aversive, and open to conflict (avoiding conflict at all costs). While one parent may be permissive and aversive to conflict, the other parent could be more critical, violent and vulnerable for the use of aversive Control (controls or hurts penalties and ultimately harms).

One parent might be quick to respond when its son is in a BPD crisis, while the other parent will enforce' orders' and' bordering. BPD individuals receive two distinct methods of coping. Imagine a type A male with a track record of problems and a high-ranking businessman. The buck stops. He does stuff. He solves conflicts. He hopes to make it easier for his daughter who has BPD and help her heal. He offers to help her find work and places to live, as well as rescuing her from financial ruin. If his daughter gets into a fight with his dad, his solutions to the problem are completely contrary to his wife's.

It fails when he applies his theory on his BPD kid. Instead of changing, it only gets worse. His wife feels he is keeping them from seeing the natural effects of his wife's actions in solving all the family problems. His wife resists any attempt to make his daughter suffer because his tactics would prevail. This is despite the fact that his wife is often subject to the child's abuse. He doesn't want to admit that he doesn't have control over a situation. His wife will not accept him being against a situation he cannot control. She has conducted extensive research into BPD, met with experts and is well-informed. She hopes her child will help her support and recommend her to see a therapist following the principles of Dialectic Behavior Therapy. Her efforts to safeguard her daughter against constant abuse from her husband and to help her daughter get past her problems are invalidated by his actions.

Each partner believes he has the best coping strategy and would succeed if the other helped him. Their power struggle and perceived invalidation resulted in ongoing disputes. This mindset gap leads to seismic disturbances which undermine the fundamental foundation of their relationships. BPD can be triggered or broken by the parents' anger and feeling of failure. This couple may be at risk of divorcing.

In the case of a mentally ill child, blame can play an important role in a parent's daily life. Working mother may feel that this would never have happened if she had stayed home with her child. The mother may believe she has always been the cause of the disease, but she might be wrong. If she had gone on to work, it would have been a different situation. The less strict parent may feel that they should have been stricter, imposed greater laws, and set higher limits. However, the controlled parent is responsible to not giving the child any more "space." BPD can be blamed on the divorced parent. However, the adopted parents are responsible for not giving the child more "space". Parents often feel guilty because they believe that something they did or did not do could have prevented the trouble.

Parents will get responses like "you overreact! It's just a normal teenage activity!" Are rages as well as mood changes and aggression indicative of impulsive or traditional youth rebellions? Do extreme circumstances warrant such a passionate response? A BPD-afflicted teenager is trying to cope with his emotional pains and depression, but he doesn't know what he can do to make it better. It is a good motivator to have the support of his peers and adhere to social standards.

Opioids, alcohol (or sexual promiscuity), reckless, dangerous, and impulsive behaviour are some of the most common ways to treat pain. While you might be concerned for the safety of your child, it's okay to be concerned about trivial problems. The secret message is that your reactions can be "excessive," insufficient, severe or both. You are seen as normalizing, making an illness out of nothing. To simplify the way you will react to this dangerous and challenging BPD, you are encouraged not to trust your instincts. This is a difficult strain to overcome. "She'll be out from a career, so everything's going to be okay." "As soon she meets somebody, she'll feel fine." It's just part of life. If you see it as this from one parent, and the other doesn't, it's going to be a bumpy ride. You need to be able to handle the situation on your own while also defending your answers from the other parent.

TARA helps families who feel their child may be suffering from BPD. They can call the help-line at 1-800-TARA. DSM-IV's review of ten year ago found that BPD was not a diagnosis for adults before 18 years. They had a 'bar mitzvah' psychological at 18 and were then confirmed as BPD sufferers. The DSM IV -TR has made it clear that BPD can be diagnosed in adults or children if symptoms last for at most one year. Many doctors are not familiar with the DSM IV TR, or they don't know how to treat BPD among children and teens. Many young people get misdiagnosed and are left behind in the mental system. Parents often feel confused because they haven't tested their symptoms. However, they know that there is something wrong. They are not well-known. Unfortunately, they have no reputation. Early intervention and accessing treatment will likely prevent the development of unwanted pregnancies and drug abuse. The lack of evidence-based medicine in many cultures, and the inability to diagnose teens can have a devastating effect. It can be dangerous today to fail to diagnose and manage youth. BPD is poorly understood by school counselors. As a result, the school curriculum fails to address the needs for young people with this condition. A pupil's maladaptive behavior is often considered a problem in school. Many parents send their teens into highly structured wildlife programs in order to control their teens' actions and keep them safe. These services and residential treatment facilities are often expensive and can't teach youth how they should manage their impulsive behaviors and solve problems. Although adolescents can sometimes do well with therapy, they are quick to fall back to old and dangerous habits once they return home.

Because of their violent coping methods, many young adults end up in juvenile jail. Paula has diagnosed her eighteen year-old daughter Lilly with BPD. Lilly spent most of the four years she was hospitalized, many times in solitary confinement. Lilly was always able to drink alcohol, even while she was being treated in hospital. Lilly's depression, and BPD were not treated by the various hospitals. What had happened to this sensitive, intelligent young woman who was sequestered and restricted? Lilly couldn't cope with her emotions without alcohol, which was why none of her hospitalizations helped. She was unable to learn how she survived outside of hospital, so it is a vicious cycle. Both her parents, both medical doctors, immediately took her to a hospital for people suffering from BPD. Unfortunately, she became addicted to alcohol and was once more abused at the hospital. She was placed in isolation and restraint. The doctor deemed her diagnosis too complicated and released Lilly without providing a treatment plan. The parents asked "Who's going after Lilly?" What support are you offering to our daughter? It was agreed that Lilly's BPD would be handled if there were no more depression symptoms. Lilly was treated like a squatter girl. Her parents were left home alone to deal with Lilly.

Siblings with BPD

The mental healthcare community failed to see the BPD siblings and brothers. BPD and sibling relationships are not the subject of any significant research. BPD can leave siblings feeling confused and impacted by their sibling's behavior. Siblings might also be exposed to a dysfunctional family, which may have had to deal with the many issues that BPD causes. BPD affects a sibling or brother and can cause a "black hole" in the home. This means that their needs are often ignored, even when they are grown. Their achievements and accomplishments are not worthy of the praise and attention they deserve. This is because their parents have become too preoccupied with keeping their sibling safe from BPD, and then putting the "crisis on the fires of day" to sleep. The siblings should be fine and healthy and do the right thing in order to compensate for their siblings' mistakes. Your parents may be struggling, and you don't wish to add to their stress. The siblings feel under pressure to be "complete," in the same way that their family pathologies affect their normality. They may be angry at their BPD sibling because of their parents' suffering. You may see them rebelling or passively expressing anger.

If children have similar personalities, it is possible for siblings to display risky or unusual behavior. This can confuse friends and family members in the classroom and in the community. This can be enough to cause anger and resentment to keep the whole family away. BPD siblings have many siblings that are responsible for taking care. Their parents are often older and they don't have the ability to live their own lives well. Accept that your parents must pass away. Siblings also face difficult decisions about whether they will be loyal to their parents or if they will be committed to the BPD brothers or sisters they love, especially if their BPD brother's oldest. We are constantly battling with an emotional diet full of tension, ambivalence, and tension as we try to live with adult relationships that cause us distress.

How is it possible that children brought up in the same home can have so many similarities and yet achieve such different outcomes? Barbara, a lovely, well-adjusted young girl, has a BPD older sibling who is also heroin dependent. Barbara thinks she won the lottery by inheriting the family gene. It is not the fault my sister for not being given the right genetics. Barbara joined her parents at the TARA DBT workshop when she was 15. With the assistance of TARA she has created a Sibling Curriculum. This curriculum teaches teens appropriate coping techniques and gives them the chance to express grievances and feelings. Barbara's observations have informed siblings about the topic. Another family has 2 children who are very close and their BPD child has been separated for over 10 years. One family has seven happy children. All seven of their children have completed TARA courses to help support their sister with BPD. She is alone and feels alienated, despite the support she has received from her brothers.

What Families Have to Know

After a while it may be difficult to spot if someone has BPD. Because of their unstable and maladaptive coping, it becomes relational. Is the first thing the chicken or is it the egg? Are these the same family behaviors? Or was this a pattern that the family has been doing all along? The clinician must meet the family during this stage. Usually, the family is in the middle an epic family crisis. To make a difference, you'll need to fully understand the condition as well as the emotions, pains, confusions, and disappointments that you experienced when dealing with your loved one suffering from BPD. It is possible to lessen your anxiety and stress by understanding BPD. Accept that your loved ones are exhibiting dangerous and dysregulated behaviors, and you cannot fix them. You have to face the facts and accept that you cannot solve your loved one's dangerous behavior. To understand that you are a busy member of the family who is trying their best, you will need the support and encouragement of your close friends and relatives.

This could be a reminder that they need to know about BPD. The sufferings that you have endured over the years will help you to understand and deal with the loss you and your family members have due to BPD. Understanding and supporting the grief felt by BPD families is essential. The psychiatric profession often fails or doesn't recognize their hardships. Families and friends must recognize the continued trauma you endured. Sometimes, it's impossible to do anything beyond what you are doing now. You are too stressed by the incessant effort and energy you put into dealing with the actions and symptoms your dear friends are causing. Your practice has been "on-call", 24 hours a week, for many years. Few practitioners could keep such a complete schedule. You spend probably more time with the BPD person that anyone else. You feel burnt out but your desires don't always come true. You feel isolated, exhausted and depressed.

BPD support groups offer emotional support to help you realize that you are not the only one dealing with this condition. Other people have also experienced similar difficulties and have made positive changes in their lives. Reading success stories and changing lives is essential. This is vital and essential. Many of the traumatic situations discussed in this book could have avoided or been minimized if BPD patients were correctly diagnosed and treated with evidence-based therapies. Family members also had to be informed about the appropriate interventions and how to improve them. Families will start to see the benefits and make changes. Although your loved one was not intentionally hurt by BPD, there is a good chance that mistakes were made. Breast milk is an essential part of infant nutrition.

In every culture, including the animal kingdom and the world, infants latch onto their mothers' breasts as soon as they come out of the womb. This is because milk keeps them healthy and stable. If you refused to give milk to your child, then you'd be called a cruel and neglectful father. You are giving your child milk if you think milk would be beneficial to the child. Include milk in the children's food, including their snacks, meals, sauces/cereals, and soups. If you feel like you're doing the best for your infant, then you can add yogurt, butter ice cream, cheese sheep, goat's milk, and cheese to their diet. No matter how good your intentions may be, your child will eventually get sick. Unbeknownst to you, milk is the main cause of rashes. Your doctor may not have mentioned that your baby might be lactose sensitive (lactose allergic). Are you a bad parent? Would you give your child milk if you knew that she was allergic to it? Regardless of your love and concern for the child, everything you do seems to bring more pain to them. You did the wrong thing again and again, but for the right reasons.

Chapter 19: Chronotherapy, Sleep Deprivation And Melatonin

Chronotherapy, which refers the shifting of your sleeping pattern, is one of our more unusual techniques. It may seem strange to adjust or shift your sleep routine, especially when it comes to mental disorders. While this is often true, it does have many benefits in helping people suffering from bipolar disorder. As with most treatments, the primary benefit is to be a proficient mood stabilizer. We'll examine here how chronotherapy and the shifting of sleep hours can help to regulate mood. And how that regulation creates a better quality of life.

There are several methods to change your sleeping time according the chronotherapy method. You can choose to sleep earlier or later, more or less. Each individual will have a different sleeping pattern, but this type of therapy just means that your normal sleeping habits are being changed. To help you change these habits, you can create a rigid schedule. It will have two benefits. One, it is capable of regulating the sleep-wake rhythm. It is also known to have a control over light-dark rhythms. These all have been shown in bipolar patients to make them happier and have mood stabilizing properties. But this is only possible if the sleep schedule can be controlled. A rigid, strict schedule will allow you to have the control you want.

To help you fall asleep, it is a good idea to take medication when trying to set up a certain sleep schedule. There are many ways to do this, but the most effective is melatonin. Melatonin, chemically known as N-acetyl-5-methoxytryptamine, is a naturally occurring hormone that helps regulate the light-dark cycle in living organisms. It can be an effective sleep aid due to this. In order to help you fall asleep, melatonin aids can be extremely helpful. When you do take melatonin orally (either capsules, tablets or liquid), it is best to take 3-6mg. This is especially useful for anyone suffering from melatonin shortage. This medication should not be taken after 9 PM.

Another important aspect of chronotheraputic care is sleep deprivation. Actively participating in sleep deprived can have less-than desirable results, just as it can with shifting your sleeping schedule. These effects, which are covered later, may be worth it if sleep deprivation or chronotherapy is shown to improve your mental health. The treatment of depression is known to be sleep deprivation. Depression can be caused by bipolar disorder. While it might seem odd, refusing to sleep can help reverse some of these negative symptoms.

When you use sleep deprivation, it's best to slow down and take shorter and shorter amounts of sleep. Both sleep deprivation types can be helpful in reducing depression. The first is partial sleep deprived. Partial sleep deprivation doesn't mean that the patient stops sleeping, but instead only has short sleep cycles every night. These periods are usually between 3-4 hours long and serve as a way to lose some sleep but still get some rest. The most severe form of sleep disruption is total sleep lack. This involves the patient not sleeping for long periods. This method can cause sleep avoidance to last up to 40-hours and may even last several days.

It is possible for your body to be tired after 40 hours of not sleeping. However, in order to minimize the effects of sleep deprivation on your body each awake period is followed with what is known as a "recovery sleep". This is a longer amount of sleep, which allows your body to get rest. Multiple studies, as well small studies, have documented the effects of sleep deprivation. 2013; 150:707). Researchers have shown that sleep deprived individuals can have mullti-modal effects on mood. This includes an impact on the levels of thyroid hormones. It can also affect metabolic and monoaminergic functions. These and other benefits were noticed more in bipolar disorder sufferers who received the treatment, than in those who didn't.

Participating in sleep deprivation can lead to fatigue and stress, which can then cause additional stress. The majority of side effects are mild, but many focus on the seriousness of the treatment. These effects include headache, fatigue. gastrointestinal symptoms, sleepiness, worsening of depression, or hypomania in patients who are vulnerable. While some may feel uncomfortable, it is important to seek out the best treatment for your condition. All methods will have side effects, but the best one for you is one that treats your symptoms.

Sources : Ravindranet Al., Journal of Affective Disorders. 2013; 150:707

Color Therapy

The next method of treatment has no side effects unlike the ones mentioned above. Certain forms of treatment are designed to treat bipolar disorder. These can come in a variety of forms and be very efficient. This section will discuss color therapy.

Color therapy is an alternative to chronotherapy and is a non-invasive method of treating bipolar disorder. The difference is that this uses colors rather than trying to use your insomnia as a form therapy. This therapy is based around the human body's natural reactions to certain colors. It is a known fact that all colors have some sort of effect on the human psyche. This effect triggers a certain response within your nervous system and brain. These are the basis of color therapy.

Color therapy is a simple way to manage the effects of bipolar disorder. There are very few side effects and it has low backlash. People who find color therapy to be helpful can use it. The goal of color therapy is to change the way things look in your everyday life. This can help to stabilize your mood.

The most important thing about color therapy is to know which colors can incite which moods. Every color is not going to make you feel the exact way you want. It is crucial to find the right method for you. For example, colors such as green, violets, pinks, and blue can have a tranquilizing effect on your brain. These are best for relaxation. Red and other colors can produce more passionate or stronger reactions. The effects of darker colors, such as purple and black, can be calming, while orange can inspire success.

After you've learned the benefits of different colors on mood, start incorporating those colors into your everyday, normal life. It is important to surround yourself with objects that will stabilize your mood. This will allow you to feel the best you can. If you need to feel passionate, ensure that the objects in your life are red. If you want calm and peaceful, use blues, greens, or other colors. This is especially important for two spaces in your daily life. This is the case for your home. The space will feel more cozy and relaxing if it has certain colors. You will feel relaxed and at ease in a place where you can feel secure. The workplace is the second important space in which color is important. If a certain color is helpful in stabilizing you, then you should try to integrate it into your work space. Decoration or simple ornaments could be used to accomplish this. You can also use the color that is most beneficial to you if your workspace isn't decorated.

Clothing is an important aspect of life. It can help to regulate your mood. Clothing is a great tool for this because it is something that you always have and is always in your environment. You can keep your head level and be reasonable in work environments by using clothing color therapy. This constant exposure to a specific color can reduce manic symptoms, as well as other benefits.

Color therapy is an excellent alternative medication. You should know that there are many medication-free treatment options available for those with bipolar disorder. Color therapy not only has no side effects but is also very simple to implement. It is easy to simply buy or locate items that contain a number of different colors. This type therapy can be implemented on your own. It is easy to learn about the colors you use and how they affect you.

Dark Therapy

The next section of this article will focus on a treatment similar to chronotherapy. This therapy, commonly called dark therapy, induces long periods or sleep but does not cause long-term sleep. Instead, it uses long periods and darkness to treat bipolar disorder. This practice is particularly useful for those with mania episodes.

Dark therapy works in the same way as chronotherapy to control bipolar disorder. This is done by controlling both the light-dark rhythms and the wake-sleep cycle. The therapeutic benefits to being submerged under total darkness are the central focus of this treatment. This can be done at any time, but most people are exposed to at least 14 hours. The rest, just like chronotherapy, is also used. Rest usually lasts between 6 p.m. - 8 a.m.

Dark therapy is beneficial for many reasons. Because it increases melatonin, the first reason is obvious. Bipolar disorder patients might have issues with melatonin release, which can lead to a decrease in sleep quality. Bipolar disorder patients are also more sensitive to the light. This is one reason why dark therapy can be so beneficial in managing mania and other bipolar symptoms. Patients with bipolar disorder may be affected by uncontrolled exposure to artificial lighting and sleep disruption caused by multiple stimuli. This type is another method to manage the wake-sleep/light–dark rhythms. This helps stabilize moods.

Dark therapy is made up of two distinct parts. The first is actually promoting a more peaceful night, which can lead to better sleep at nights. These benefits can be many, and we will cover them all below. Other benefits include helping to regulate mood via a controlled exposure of light. You can control the timing of light exposure, which can be helpful for those with bipolar disorder.

One study (Barbini et al., Bipolar Disorders. 2005, 7 :98. The authors looked at how dark therapy could help those suffering from bipolar disorder. Researchers studied 32 patients suffering from the disorder. The patients received dark therapy as well as their regular treatments. Analyses were conducted over a 2-week period. Participants who had been receiving dark therapy underwent 14-hour cycles. The results of the analysis showed that the treatment was highly effective in helping control and treat mania. This was due to the factors mentioned above. Patients who used dark therapy in combination with traditional medicine slept better than those who did not use medicine. This is a strong indicator that dark therapy can induce better sleep.

Sleeplessness, also known as restlessness while sleeping, can cause many problems. It is easier to overcome the negative effects of the light-dark rhythm by controlling it. Dark therapy reduces mood swings and other symptoms. Although dark therapy is not recommended for use alone, it can be effective in combination with other treatments. Practitioners have been able to combine antidepressant drugs with light therapy, sleep-wake patterns manipulations, and antidepressant drugs in recent years. This has allowed them to develop new tools for rapid and sustained antidepressant responses. It is not necessary for dark therapy success, but this is a great example of how dark therapy can be used to its maximum potential.

Even though it may seem strange, there have never been any side effects from dark therapy. Though it may seem that dark therapy can cause side effects, as this treatment is based upon sleep, there are no such negative effects. Dark therapy can be an effective way to deal with manic episodes. Dark therapy is also a great option if your insomnia or other sleep issues are affecting your daily life. You should not use dark therapy as an alternative to traditional treatment.

Diet

Similar to many other treatments, bipolar disorder is affected by the diet. A particular diet can be very helpful in managing symptoms. The ketogenic or low-carb diet will be discussed. It can be used to treat bipolar disorder. A ketogenic lifestyle, just like all diets, requires that you change the way you eat. A ketogenic diet, unlike any other, attempts to force certain tissue types to switch to a primary fuel source. One of these tissues is brain. Therefore, it can be used for treating disorders that revolve around the brain such as bipolar disorder. In that it alters nerve activity, which can have calming/ relaxing effects, a ketogenic diet could be very important. These effects can also be used to decrease distress, which can make bipolar disorder worse.

A ketogenic diet reduces carbohydrate intake while consuming high levels fat and sufficient protein. This will help achieve the main goal of the diet which is to maintain either a fasting or starving metabolic rate over a longer period of times. This process eliminates glucose from your daily diet. In this way, when glucose from the digestion of carbohydrates is no longer present, your liver produces ketone bodies by partially burning fatty acids. This is how your liver switches the fuel you use. The liver produces ketones which are remnants fatty acids. These remaining fatty acids are released into the bloodstream to be used for fuel.

It is possible to affect amino acid metabolism if there is an increase of ketones in your brain. This refers a rise in the amino acid glutamic, which then becomes a different type, known as gamma–aminobutryic. GABA levels that are high make nerve cells less exitable. This is because it controls certain functions within the body.

Although it is best known for treating epilepsy-related children, the ketogenic lifestyle may also be useful for people with bipolar disorder. The ketogenic treatment can also be used to treat epilepsy. What does a seizure trigger have to do the bipolar disorder Bipolar disorder sufferers don't often experience seizures. But, many treatments for this disorder increase the seizure trigger. These treatments may range from anticonvulsant medication, to electroconvulsive Therapy. Given this correlation, it makes sense that a ketogenic diet can be helpful in managing bipolar disorder.

A ketogenic diet may be able help those suffering from bipolar disorder by stabilizing their moods and giving them greater control. It is unclear why this happens and what the therapeutic benefits of the ketogenic lifestyle are. It could be the presence or stabilization in blood sugar. These benefits could also be due to the decrease in blood sugar, insulin, or any combination thereof.

This article will focus on a study that examined the effects and effectiveness of the ketogenic treatment for bipolar disorder. This 2013 study was published on the Nuerocase journal. The study was published in 2013 by Nuerocase. It involved two women diagnosed with type 2 Bipolar Disorder, which is a subset of the disorder that has more episodes of depression and less manic episodes. These meats were pork, chicken, seafood, and beef. They also restricted themselves to oil and cream, which are fattier. Both women continued with this diet for 2-3 years. They saw positive changes in both cases. The women both experienced mood stabilization that was much better and they had very little to no negative side effects. This is another example illustrating the health benefits of a ketogenic Diet.

While the above study didn't show any adverse effects for the women, it does not mean that the ketogenic lifestyle should be avoided. You can experience changes in your regular diet that have negative consequences for your body. Many people will experience fatigue and sluggishness upon starting the ketogenic Diet. This is normal and may become more prominent here. There may also be side effects. A few minor side effects may include constipation or dehydration as well as electrolyte, micronutrient, and vitamin deficiencies. But, there are more serious complications to the ketogenic lifestyle. These complications include kidney stones, high cholesterol, and other serious health issues. Also, it is possible for bone fractures to occur and gall bladder issues to develop. It is important to exercise caution when following this diet.

Chapter 20: Staying Well And Thriving In Your Life

Bipolar illness can sometimes make life difficult. It can take a lot out of you and it can cause severe depression. -Carrie Fisher[32]

It is crucial to develop a plan of wellness for your well-being as well as overall improvement in managing the bipolar disorder. Without a plan for action, you can't expect to make progress. A plan of action will allow you to achieve your health and wellness goals. You can't assume things will happen. You have to think about and reflect on what is possible. These are some tips that will help you improve your condition. These are my top tips.

Your doctor should continue to monitor your progress.

First, you must realize that finding the right physician is an essential part to your wellness plan. Your doctor should listen to what you have to say and give you information and support to help with your bipolar disorder. Call your doctor right away if you feel unwell. You should also dial your doctor immediately if you feel that you are on the brink of mania.

Any abnormality you notice should be reported promptly to your doctor. Trust that your doctor is there to help you and to be your ally. For your ongoing health, make sure to schedule regular visits with your doctor. Have him check on your medication levels in order to ensure that it is working properly.

Do not stop taking your medication. Relapses into mania and depression can occur if you stop taking the drug suddenly. Why so many people go to the hospital or relapse is because they think they don't really need the medication and stop taking it. Then they become unstable, and are unable to cope with the symptoms associated with mania. They become agitated and have racing thoughts that lead to mania.

You should follow the prescribed program to keep yourself healthy and out hospital. If your doctor feels it is necessary to adjust your medication, or change any other aspect of your treatment plan, he will.

Healthy Eating

Part of a healthy lifestyle is eating well. For optimal health, it is essential to think about how you can eat right. By making small adjustments to your diet you can prevent depressive episodes or manic symptoms. It will pay off in the long term to maintain a healthy lifestyle. Although it will not cure you, it will help you to remain healthy. These foods are good for you to include in your daily routine. [33]

1. Whole grain food

Whole grain foods can be good for your stomach and heart. They also help make serotonin. This helps you relax and feels good. Whole grain foods are breads, pastas, oatmeal, quinoa, brown rice and bread. Get in on the benefits of whole grains to improve your health.

2. Diverse types of fish

Different types of fish can be beneficial to your brain. The Omega-3 fatty acids can be beneficial for your heart, too. You should add fish to your meal plan.

3. Turkey

Enjoy Thanksgiving turkey and find that you feel more sleepy afterward. It stimulates the production of serotonin. This helps to relax your body and improves your sleep quality at night. You might be able reverse the effects of depression if you have higher levels of serotonin.

4. Nuts

Magnesium can also be obtained from nuts. Studies have shown that nearly half the Americans don't eat enough magnesium, which can cause them stress.

[34] Peanuts (cashews), almonds, and cashews can be good for mania. They help regulate your cortisol levels and make your nervous systems work well.

5. Probiotics

Probiotics are beneficial bacteria that help to regulate emotions. They include milk and yogurt as well as sauerkraut, miso, kimchi, and sauerkraut. Regular intake of probiotics will help to keep stress levels in check.

6. Dark chocolate

Everyone loves to eat chocolate. One study by the Journal of Proteome Research suggests that eating a quarter of an ounce of dark chocolate per day can lower stress levels (Healthline).

7. Herbal tea

Chamomile is a type tea that can be used to soothe anxiety, insomnia, and stomachaches (Healthline). It has also been found to help with depression symptoms. You can also feel better with hot water. However, chamomile is known to be especially soothing for stress-related feelings.

8. Beans

The magnesium in beans can make it a great food. Magnesium is known to help manage mania symptoms and improve mood. It's a good idea that you include these foods in the diet.

Foods to Avoid

While experiencing manic episodes, you need to be careful about what foods you eat. Avoid caffeine if your mood is euphoric. You shouldn't drink five cups of coffee every morning, as this can lead to anxiety. Avoid excessive alcohol consumption as it can cause depression symptoms. It can cause dehydration and poor sleep quality at night. Although it can help with symptoms of mania and other disorders, it can also cause problems.

You may also want to avoid certain foods (Healthline).

* Smoked or processed meats

* Fermented foods such kimchi, sauerkraut, and sauerkraut

* Soybeans

* Dry fruit (Healthline).

You might also avoid foods high on sugar or fat because these can be very unhealthy and cause weight gain. Your treatment plan may also be affected by these foods.

Get regular sleep

As we mentioned, sleep is the key to wellness. Proper sleep is the key to your stability, and not going insane. The goal should be to get between seven and nine hours sleep per night. [35]

Stress can be reduced in your life

If there are many stressors in life, it is possible to suffer from many issues. This can impact your mood and lead you to be more aggressive. It can trigger depression or madness and cause you to feel anxious. You should restrict your access to anything that is causing stress. This includes relationships and technology. Facebook is known to cause stress and anxiety. Limit your social media use. Depending on how you use it, technology can either be very helpful or very destructive. You should limit your screen time. You must find the right balance to avoid falling off the edge.

Conclusion

Bipolar disorder can usually be treated and contained with proper and effective treatment. Every person is different and therefore treatment and therapy should be customized. There are many resources beyond the medical side. Patients are strongly advised to consult a healthcare professional immediately to obtain a proper diagnosis and assistance in choosing the best method of treatment.

Remember that you are not powerless when you deal with bipolar disorder. You must be able and able to manage your stress levels. Accepting your bipolar disorder and having a firm grasp of reality will be a big help. It is not a good idea to spend time wishing for a cure.

Always remember that there is light at every end of the tunnel. This is why it is important to do more research and reach out to those who are needed. The more you understand about the illness, then the better. You must have a better understanding of the disease to be able manage it and its treatments.

You should avoid becoming dependent for bipolar disorder. Patients are often dependent on others when they are informed that they have a mental illness.

Understanding that you have a mental health condition is not an easy task can make it much more manageable. Sometimes you may feel like your life is a constant struggle. Some days and nights will be more difficult than other. But don't give up. Know when to stop, take a break, and remember to enjoy your day.

Bipolar disorder can be described as a mental illness that is similar to a physical problem.

It is important to be self-aware, critical and objective about your surroundings and others. You must be analytical and sensitive to your surroundings and those around you.

This is how you can win this war.

You can trust that the information in this book will provide you with helpful tips and useful instructions that will allow you to cross the threshold into treatment and acceptance.

I will however reiterate that this book shouldn't be your only recourse for treatment, support, or advice.

If you feel like you are experiencing bipolar disorder, don't hesitate to reach out and speak to a professional or close friend.

Talking to someone about your feelings can make it easier. Sometimes people are the best form of medicine.